Life in Medieval Europe: Fact and Fiction

Life in Medieval Europe: Fact and Fiction

Danièle Cybulskie

First published in Great Britain in 2019 by
Pen and Sword History
An imprint of
Pen & Sword Books Ltd
Yorkshire - Philadelphia

Copyright © Danièle Cybulskie, 2019

ISBN 9781526733450

The right of Danièle Cybulskie to be identified as Author of this work has been asserted by her in accordance with the Copyright, Designs and Patents Act 1988.

A CIP catalogue record for this book is available from the British Library.

All rights reserved. No part of this book may be reproduced or transmitted in any form or by any means, electronic or mechanical including photocopying, recording or by any information storage and retrieval system, without permission from the Publisher in writing.

Typeset in INDIA By IMPEC e Solutions

Printed and bound in the UK by TJ International Ltd.

Pen & Sword Books Ltd incorporates the Imprints of Pen & Sword Books Archaeology, Atlas, Aviation, Battleground, Discovery, Family History, History, Maritime, Military, Naval, Politics, Railways, Select, Transport, True Crime, Fiction, Frontline Books, Leo Cooper, Praetorian Press, Seaforth Publishing, Wharncliffe and White Owl.

For a complete list of Pen & Sword titles please contact

PEN & SWORD BOOKS LIMITED
47 Church Street, Barnsley, South Yorkshire, S70 2AS, England
E-mail: enquiries@pen-and-sword.co.uk
Website: www.pen-and-sword.co.uk

or

PEN AND SWORD BOOKS
1950 Lawrence Rd, Havertown, PA 19083, USA
E-mail: Uspen-and-sword@casematepublishers.com
Website: www.penandswordbooks.com

Contents

Introduction		viii
Chapter One	A Dirty Little Secret	1
	Did medieval people take baths?	1
	Did they ever wash their hands?	4
	Did they use soap?	5
	What about their teeth?	6
	Did they wash their clothes?	7
	Were the cities filthy?	9
	What about toilets?	11
Chapter Two	Farming, Fasting, Feasting	14
	What did people eat?	14
	Didn't everyone just cook their meals at home?	16
	Wasn't the food all bland?	17
	How far did the trade routes stretch?	18
	Did Europeans have a lot of contact with different cultures?	19
	What did people drink?	19
	Were they constantly drunk?	21
	Was everyone up for a night of drunken excitement?	22
	What was a feast like?	23
	Did they really eat with their hands?	25
	Did people have any table manners?	26
	Did they have dessert?	27
	Wasn't some of that a little unhygienic?	28

Chapter Three	The Art of Love	31
	Did medieval people date?	31
	Weren't all of the marriages arranged?	33
	How did they get married?	34
	What about the wedding night?	36
	What about their sex lives?	36
	What about LGBTQIA+ people?	38
	Even priests were having sex?	41
	People were using contraceptives?	42
	Did they love their children?	43
	What was childhood like?	45
	Did everyone die young?	47
	How did people cope with death?	48
	What actually happened when someone died?	49
Chapter Four	Nasty and Brutish	53
	Wasn't the whole political structure of the Middle Ages based on 'might is right'?	53
	There were slaves in medieval Europe?	54
	When a serf got married, did the lord get to sleep with the bride?	55
	Weren't punishments always pretty brutal?	56
	What about executions?	57
	How did trial by combat and trial by ordeal work?	58
	How did the justice system work after that?	59
	They used forensic evidence?	61
	If people didn't confess to their crimes, were they tortured?	62
	Weren't medieval people always fighting?	63
	Was the longbow really that deadly?	64

	What about crossbows?	65
	What about knights?	65
	Could they even move under all that armour?	67
	Did knights get to use their skills often?	68
	How did a siege work?	68
	What is a trebuchet?	69
	What else did besiegers do to get in?	70
	Did anyone fight pitched battles?	72
	Were guns invented in the Middle Ages?	73
Chapter Five	The Age of Faith	75
	Was medieval Europe ruled by the church?	75
	How did people practice their faith?	76
	Who took care of people's spiritual needs?	78
	What was it like to be a monk or a nun?	79
	Weren't monasteries also schools?	80
	Weren't there a lot of stories about saints in the Middle Ages?	81
	Did many people go on pilgrimages?	83
	Did everyone believe?	83
	Wasn't the church always burning people for heresy?	86
	What was life like for the Jews?	87
	What about Muslims?	88
	What about the crusades?	89
Chapter Six	In Sickness and in Health	93
	What happened when people got hurt?	93
	What happened when people got sick?	94
	Did they rely solely on faith?	95
	What if they needed surgery?	96
	Did they have doctors like we do today?	98

viii Life in Medieval Europe: Fact and Fiction

	What about women's medicine?	99
	What about people with disabilities?	100
	What was the Black Death?	102
Chapter Seven	Couture, Competition, and Courtly Love	104
	What did people wear?	104
	Did they wear accessories?	106
	How did people make their clothes?	107
	Did medieval people wear underwear?	109
	What did they do for fun?	110
	Did they listen to music?	111
	Did they play games?	113
	Did they play any sports?	114
	What about tournaments?	115
	Did anyone read for pleasure?	117
A Final Word		121
Acknowledgements		122
Bibliography		123
Notes		133
Index		136

Introduction

Before this book ever became real enough to stare at me in the form of a blinking cursor, it was an idea I'd had based on dozens of conversations with friends and strangers alike. Having been a medievalist for quite a few years now, I've noticed that whenever people are drawn into a piece of historical fiction – or a great story from history, itself – we naturally tend to ask ourselves the same questions about the time period in which it takes place. These questions are all based around the human element: what was it like to *be* there and to experience that moment in time?

While we may learn about dates and kings and wars in history classes, it seems that too often we miss out on those little details that made up ordinary life. And yet those are the details that bring history into full colour, the details that connect us as human beings through time, and the details that stick with us long after we've closed a book or turned off a screen.

This book looks at medieval Europe in terms of those little itches of human curiosity that may not be scratched by a conventional look at history. Not everything that you might expect from a regular book about the Middle Ages is in here, but many things that you may not have thought to wonder about are. You'll find that much of what we explore pulls the Middle Ages back from the extremes for which it is known: extreme violence, extreme filth, extreme prejudice. Barbara Tuchman famously called the fourteenth century 'a distant mirror', but I've found that the mirror is not as distant as it may seem.

For our purposes, we'll be looking at medieval Europe from around 500 CE to around 1500 CE. This roughly corresponds to the fall of the Roman Empire and the rise of Protestantism. Naturally, no one at the time thought of these markers as distinctions of a historical era called 'the medieval period', but they're helpful markers, nonetheless. As Roman influence began to fall away, new power structures arose in the shape of what has been called (and argued and debated) feudalism, while at the other end of the period, Protestantism meant a break with the power of the Catholic church, and a different kind of independence for European kingdoms.

A lot can happen in a thousand years, and a lot did happen. Empires rose and fell, technology leapt forward, and half the population was wiped out in the course of a single year. We won't be able to cover it all in such a short book (or even a thousand short books), so there will be quite a lot of necessary generalising. My hope is that this book will whet your appetite enough that you'll read on and investigate whatever tickles your fancy, from Vikings to Venetians.

While our focus will be on medieval Europe, it's important to remember that this was just one small part of a wide world, and that there was a whole lot of fascinating stuff going on at the same time elsewhere. Europe was connected to a vast network of travel and trade that stretched from Greenland down the Nile and east to China. Goods, stories, and people made their way across thousands of miles slowly, with millions of tiny, human interactions along the way, making the medieval world culturally much richer and more diverse than people once believed. I ask you to imagine medieval Europe not as a place where everyone looked, dressed, and behaved the same way (they didn't), but as a place where peoples and cultures mixed and collided. I also invite you to read further, both geographically and historically, and learn more about what other amazing and wonderful things were going on around the world at this time.

So, what was life like in medieval Europe? It's often been described as 'nasty, brutish, and short' (à la Thomas Hobbes), as 'the age of faith', and a time in which people would rather die than take a bath. As we'll see, there are some grains of truth to these notions, although they've tended to be magnified through our need to believe we've come a long way in the time since. In reality, medieval people had much the same dreams, desires, and expectations that we do, and they reveal themselves to us through their daily habits, advice, and leisure pursuits.

History is fundamentally the story of human beings making their way through the world as best they can with curiosity, frustration, humour, and courage. It's my belief that getting to know the people of the past changes our thinking about human beings in general, and fosters understanding and compassion across boundaries. Beyond that, learning about a world that is so strange and yet so familiar is just an unbelievable amount of fun.

Chapter One

A Dirty Little Secret

One of the most common myths about the Middle Ages is that no one cared about getting clean. It's just one of those 'facts' that seems to get passed on without question, an accepted part of what we know about this era. Much is made of the filth of the period, but to be squeamish about medieval hygiene is to come from a place of enormous privilege. Not only do we know about bacteria and viruses today, but many of us have the resources to keep clean; namely, access to filtered water, heating systems, and cleaning products. Many people on Earth today don't have access to these things, and so they keep clean and healthy the best they can. The same was true for the majority of people in the Middle Ages.

Did medieval people take baths?

The answer to this is a resounding yes – and no. As the Romans slowly receded from most of Europe, they left behind the bathhouses they so enjoyed, many of them ornate and cleverly constructed to make use of natural hot springs. Both bathhouses and steam baths continued to be well-used features of towns and cities all over Europe throughout the medieval period, although perhaps not as often as we might prefer.

Bathhouses could be in the Roman style of pools in which everyone soaked together, or they could be rooms in which there were many bathtubs big enough to fit a few people at a time. Most medieval bathtubs, in both public bathhouses and private homes, generally looked like the bottom half of a wooden barrel and were made by coopers. Because it's an unpleasant feeling to get a splinter while sitting down naked, bathers would often have a linen sheet draped into the bathtub as a layer between themselves and the wood. They'd also make a linen tent above the bathtub to keep things steamy and cosy. For additional luxury, water could be sprinkled with flower petals to make the bather smell nice. Patrons had to pay a small fee to use the bathhouses, much as people today do when they visit a spa.

Evidently, people enjoyed their baths: there were dozens of bathhouses in Paris alone in the thirteenth century, and London even had a *Bathestereslane*. Bathhouses were used by both men and women, and although Christians often bathed in mixed company, occasionally they had separate times and bathhouses, as did Muslims and Jews. Concerned writers specifically warned against sharing a bath with those of other religious beliefs, as the casual social setting and lack of religious attire might lead to a dangerous mixing of beliefs.

Although it may seem strange to us, in the medieval world you could have your bath and your dinner along with it. There are many manuscript images that feature people enjoying a meal while steaming away in all their naked glory. This wasn't considered unhygienic at the time; after all, if you weren't clean in a bathhouse, where were you clean?

But bathhouses weren't just for getting clean: they were also convenient places to get dirty. Given that people routinely got naked together there, it seems inevitable that bathhouses would also become a place for sexual rendezvous, and this is exactly what happened. While some establishments offered food for the bathers, others also provided beds – and prostitutes. Eventually, they gained a very bad reputation, indeed, and the common English word for bathhouse – 'stew' – became synonymous with brothel. In 1417, the London aldermen banned stews on the grounds that they were places of every kind of immorality. The fact that the ban specifically excluded personal baths suggests that people did have their own bathtubs, and that not everyone was using bathing as an excuse for promiscuity: some people were actually getting clean. Londoners were so unimpressed with the ban on their bathing that the aldermen were made to backtrack only eleven years later on the condition that bathhouse owners promised (and paid a bond to seal the deal) that they would run 'honest stews'.

People in rural areas bathed in lakes, rivers, and streams, and even the urban poor who were not able to afford a visit to the bathhouse tried to get clean where they could. We know about their bathing in part because of coroners' records; sometimes people's efforts to stay clean ended in tragedy, with people young and old drowning in the process.

Though people throughout Europe were bathing wherever they could, it seems that bathing was still a relatively rare event for northern Europeans, occurring at most weekly, and at least twice a year. Muslims and Jews followed religious codes that required them to bathe more frequently, but for medieval Christians, the idea of being as clean as modern people are today was spiritually difficult to wrestle with, as they would have seen it as vanity or excessive pleasure; in other words, elevating the body over the spirit. In fact, some Christian writers criticised Muslims for bathing too frequently, as if this was an admission that they were dirtier than Christians.

Devout medieval Christians believed that the body was inherently sinful. After all, it couldn't even take a bath without lust being involved. To care too much about the body was to take time and energy away from spiritual matters, and many Christian practices of devotion stemmed from the desire to mortify the flesh and deny the body its pleasure. Fasting, self-flagellation, and the wearing of hair shirts, for example, were all meant to make the body uncomfortable, and to remind the sinner of the weakness and transience of the flesh. Being dirty also meant being uncomfortable, so some faithful people found skipping baths to be praiseworthy.

Monastic rules on bathing varied. *The Rule of St Benedict* suggests that, 'Use of baths should be offered to the sick as often as expedient, but less readily allowed to the healthy, and especially the young.' As with the public bathhouses, this reluctance to allow younger monks regular baths had more to do with concerns around celibate young men being naked together than cleanliness. The ideal monastic community outlined in the ninth-century Plan of St Gall also specifies 'separate bathhouses ... for the novices, the abbot, and the monks, as well as the sick.' Although there are evident moral concerns around bathing, the implication is that everyone in the monastery was expected to bathe.

The monks at Westminster Abbey were definitely not averse to bathing: the abbey had its very own bath attendant.

> Bathhouses, brewhouses, and bakeries sometimes shared walls and resources to make better use of the heat they both needed.

England's King John didn't seem to mind having servants get themselves sweaty carrying buckets of heated water up and down stairs to fill his bath; apparently he even had a servant, by the name of William, who was specifically set in charge of the king's bathtub. A few generations later, Edward III was no doubt praised by his own servants when he decided to make his bathing habit easier on everybody by installing hot and cold water taps for his own personal bathroom in Westminster Palace. When it came to bathing, being king definitely had its advantages.

As with many distasteful habits that are popularly referred to as 'medieval', you're much more likely to find advice on getting 'clean' by wiping with linen – not bathing – beginning in the sixteenth century. It was Early Modern people who began to avoid bathhouses for fear of disease, especially syphilis and plague. Before this, if a bathhouse was closed or people were warned away, it had to do with the scandalous behaviour springing from the nakedness involved.

Did they ever wash their hands?

While all-out bathing could be inconvenient for people who had the misfortune of not being kings, medieval people did require that hands and faces remained clean, especially before eating. Books of manners insisted on it as a show of good breeding and politeness, and rules for religious communities required the washing of hands both before meals and before mass. Because monks and nuns washed their hands so frequently, they sometimes installed taps for this purpose.

If you weren't lucky enough to have indoor taps, regular washing before meals might mean using a specially made urn for pouring out clean water: an aquamanile. Aquamaniles and wash bowls were decorative touches to add to the dining hall, as well as being practical. Washing the hands and face was important, so it was worth it to have wash bowls that left a good impression on guests. Linen towels would be provided for drying.

Did they use soap?

Soap was known and loved in Europe right from the beginning of the medieval period. Even those who were meant to be living an austere and strict religious life were expected to use it. As the ninth-century synods of Aachen declared, it was essential that every monk should be supplied, in addition to their clothing, with a 'sufficient amount of soap'.

Most of the soap that would have been used was lye soap made from animal fat (tallow) and wood ash, and it was used for cleaning fleece, clothes, and bodies. While lye soap is great for cutting through oil and grease, it can be harsh on the skin because of its alkaline nature. 'Black soap' had a high concentration of ash, which made it ideal for washing fleece, but uncomfortable for washing people. Those who could afford it used the much milder olive oil soap – 'white soap' – made in Italy, southern France, and Spain. *The Trotula*, a book of both medical advice and cosmetic recipes for women, encourages the use of this gentle 'French soap' for ladies washing their faces.

In Boccaccio's *Decameron* (a fourteenth-century Italian poem), one of the characters is said to use 'clove-scented' soap, which indicates that soap was being produced in different combinations to create better scents. Although it seems unlikely that most everyday washing – for example, before meals – involved soap, it nevertheless was used with enough frequency in bathing that town planners in Ypres had to ensure that the bathhouses drained away to a sewer to keep the soap from contaminating the clean water supply. This may also have had something to do with the fact that used public bathwater is just not that enjoyable to drink.

If soap was unavailable, medieval people could make use of herbs and other plants to make themselves smell better while washing. John

Russell's fifteenth-century *Boke of Nurture*, for instance, recommends both 'sweet herbs and flowers' as well as 'warm rosewater'. *The Trotula* offers a recipe for shampoo which involves 'ashes of burnt vine, the chaff of barley nodes, and licorice wood ... and sowbread', which will make a woman's hair 'golden and shimmering'. This sounds much more agreeable than the recipe for black hair which involves boiling a headless, tail-less, green lizard in oil.

It's a safe bet that the aristocracy had more access to soap, and more opportunities to use it, leaving the peasantry pretty pungent by modern standards, despite their best efforts. Still, evidence suggests that soap was more common and more frequently used in Europe in the Middle Ages than in the more oft-praised periods that came before and after it. And that is nothing to sniff at.

What about their teeth?

It's a human commonality that no one wants to speak to – let alone kiss – someone with terrible breath. This may have been the most compelling motivation for the medieval population (and arguably the modern one) to keep their teeth nice and clean.

Brushing your teeth in the Middle Ages usually meant scrubbing them with something abrasive, usually a tooth powder on your finger or a moistened cloth. Many toothpaste recipes have survived the Middle Ages, including ones which use salt and pepper, or something sweeter-smelling like sage. One Welsh recipe advises,

> Take the leaves of sage, powder with as much again of salt, and make it into balls. Bake them till they are burnt and powder. Let your teeth be rubbed frequently therewith. It will render the teeth clean, white, and sweet.

If there wasn't time enough for a full-on scrub, a person could chew cloves for a quick breath-freshener. Gilbertus Anglicus, who wrote a compendium of medicine in the thirteenth century, suggests making your own breath mints out of 'sweet-smelling spices'. He also advocated for preventative measures, such as cleaning the teeth after eating, and drinking wine spiced with hyssop, cinnamon, spikenard, or cubeb every night.

Tooth scrubs would be effective at clearing off some plaque, but not as effective at preventing cavities. Fortunately, most people's diets were relatively low in sugar, which meant that they were in far less danger for developing cavities than we are. Sugar was known in Europe, being brought home by crusaders and traders from further east, but like so many imports that had to journey across a continent, sugar was expensive – another reason it wasn't a big part of the medieval diet. It wasn't until trade with the Americas was established in the Early Modern period that sugar became a regular enough part of the common peoples' diets that it was a serious threat to dental health.

Cavities were thought to be caused by 'tooth-worms', a logical conclusion for people to make, given that they leave behind the same tiny little holes that worms do. Some cures for cavities involve luring out the tooth worms to give the patient some respite. If a tooth got to be too far gone, it would have to be removed by the local barber-surgeon. Believe it or not, there is evidence of some cavities being filled, and loose teeth being wired together.

It's not clear how many people actively took care of their teeth on a daily basis, but the evidence suggests that people were keen to have clean, white teeth for aesthetic reasons, as well as medical ones.

Did they wash their clothes?

As with bathing, doing laundry in medieval Europe took time and effort, so the frequency of washing varied. Some late medieval advice recommends changing undergarments every day, which would've required a great deal of money and work. One thirteenth-century hospital in Troyes required weekly – if not daily – washing of the sheets; another in York kept laundresses on staff to keep the linens clean. *The Rule of St Benedict* requires that every monk have 'two tunics and two cowls, because of the need to [wear] them at night and to wash them', meaning it was normal for one set of robes to be in the wash at any time. An abbey in Harrold was ordered by its bishop to ensure that a laundress washed the nuns' clothes every two or three weeks. Even armies had laundresses in the followers' camps to clean clothes, sheets, and towels.

Doing laundry involved immersing it in water, stepping on it or beating it with a stick or a 'bouke' made expressly for the purpose, scrubbing with soap (if some was available) or urine, rinsing with clean water, wringing by hand, and then drying the washing on a line or spreading it out on fragrant bushes to make it smell nice. Often, laundry was spread onto lavender bushes to infuse the cloth with their smell, so it's probably no coincidence that the plant's name is connected to the Latin word for washing ('lavare'). Sachets of dried lavender are still used to keep clothes and linens fresh today.

People in the country could wash their clothes in rivers, ponds, or lakes, or they could boil their laundry in a pot over the fire. Some cities, like Siena, had designated fountains just for laundry, with bi-laws against tradesmen using the water for their own purposes. London had a popular washing spot on the river Thames, aptly called 'Lavenderbrigge', while nurses in Paris used the Seine to wash their hospitals' sheets.

Doing laundry at home took so much time and effort that it was often easier just to get someone else to do it. Most professional medieval launderers were women, gathering washing from many households as contract work, or as an employee of a noble family or institution. Laundresses, as working women out in the street and moving from house to house, were the object of moral suspicion, often equated with prostitutes. To ward off the evils of women, some priests allowed only men to wash the holy garments and cloths associated with the mass.

Some religious communities did their own laundry, while others had their lay servants clean their clothes and sheets for them. At the monastery of Cluny, the brothers picked up their clean laundry where it was neatly set out for them in the cloister, their names carefully stitched on the inside of each robe, while two brothers supervised to prevent any squabbles. Anyone who failed to put away his own laundry was chastised.

For a privileged few, doing laundry was both profitable and high-status. After all, being privy to the literal dirty laundry of the royal family meant being privy to its figurative dirty laundry, as well. It's no wonder some royal laundresses were well paid and well cared for.

While professional laundresses no doubt had their trade secrets, ordinary people had their own. In his book of advice, Le Ménagier de Paris ('The Goodman of Paris') instructs his young wife to save a flask of verjuice expressly for stain removal. He also recommends removing oil and grease stains with urine, lye, ash, or oxgall. Storing clothing with dried roses was also a good idea to keep them smelling fresh, as people have been doing for hundreds of years both before and since.

For medieval people as for modern, there's nothing quite like the feeling of sliding into freshly-laundered sheets, even if that pleasure isn't meant to last. As the women of *The Distaff Gospels* put it, 'When you put clean sheets on a bed, the angel of God lays down between them, but as soon as someone farts or passes wind, it vanishes.'

Were the cities filthy?

In a word, yes.

Think about it: within a city, you'd have waste made by not only by thousands of people, but also by domestic animals, such as dogs, cats, and horses, as well as farm animals brought in for sale or slaughter, like sheep and cows. You'd also have those animals that we think of as being associated with farms, but that were a regular part of even a townsperson's household, such as chickens and a pig or two. The sheer number of people and animals made getting rid of a city's waste a logistical nightmare, but people really did try their best.

As you can imagine, all of the human and animal traffic (and its accompanying mess) would have made dirt roads unbelievably mucky, so one of the first priorities for cities was to cobble the streets as soon as possible. City streets were levelled with rubble or gravel, and often had a gutter in the centre of the street to keep rainwater running, washing filth away. In many cities, people were responsible for keeping the street directly in front of their home clean and in good repair, sometimes on a weekly basis, reporting damaged streets or bad drainage to the city council. Hefty fines and complaints rained down on the heads of those who didn't clean up their own messes.

Medieval homes had less garbage to get rid of on a weekly basis than we do now, as items were reused and repaired much more often, and there wasn't the same amount of disposable packaging or sheer volume of things to purchase. Kitchen scraps could be fed to animals or used as compost for a backyard garden. Rags could be used for cleaning or patches, or even woven together to make rugs; eventually, they'd be used to make paper. Parchment could be scraped to remove writing, and then reused. Broken pottery could be crushed up and used as fill for holes in the road or areas of the landscape that needed to be built up (we still often refer to dumps as 'landfills'). Still, even with all this repurposing and recycling, there would be rubbish that needed to be gotten rid of. So, where did it go?

Believe it or not, some medieval cities, like London, had street cleaners on the payroll, and regular garbage removal services for their citizens, just like today. Carters would come along weekly and collect garbage, bringing it to the city dump which would be a designated area either within or just outside of the city walls. In cities that had such regular collection, home and store owners would pay a small amount for the service. In other cities, people were responsible for bringing their own garbage to the dump site or paying private contractors to do it for them. Some cities even had civic officials walk the streets to make sure everyone had done their part.

Of course (then as now), people will take an easy route if they can, and there are complaints and bi-laws from the Middle Ages that show people dumped their garbage on vacant lots, shoved it in front of their neighbours' houses, or even took money to remove garbage only to dump it at the first opportunity. The fact that these legal documents exist demonstrates that people didn't appreciate having garbage all over their cities, and they especially didn't like stepping over waste.

Dung from the animals that were driven, ridden, or chased through the streets was a useful commodity for gardens and farms, so people would collect it from the streets and bring it to farms outside the city.

Often, carts that were used to bring produce into the city were used to cart dung out, a resourceful idea, although one that no doubt will turn many modern urban-dwellers' stomachs. If we consider that much of the produce being brought into the city was grown using dung as fertiliser, though, the idea becomes a bit less disturbing.

What about toilets?

There's a common image of people leaning out their windows tossing the contents of a chamber pot in the street, but tossing waste where people might be walking was risky business, indeed. While it's true that liquid waste could be poured into the streets to flow down the gutter, no one appreciated solid waste on the streets – especially human.

For many homeowners, there was little reason to toss the contents of a chamber pot out the window, as houses and shops often had their own latrines in the cellar or in the backyard. Many homes even had pipes leading from a garderobe inside the house to a latrine, although they were not flushed with water as they are today. There are complaints from London about particularly uncivilised people whose pipes led directly into the alley below, but these were definitely not approved of in any way. In fact, we only know about them because of an investigation into how to stop them. No doubt people learned quickly to avoid these alleys, as they did Winchester's 'Shitelane'.

Strict rules in cities like London determined where homeowners' privies could be situated, and how they should be built. The easiest option was to build your privy over a river; that way, the waste would never build up – at least, not in your own backyard. As cities grew and became more populated, however, this trick became unsustainable and went by the wayside in the face of bi-laws and fines.

Most backyard privies were meant to be lined in some fashion, either with wood or stone, to minimise seepage. Naturally, stone privies were best, but they could be expensive. Some people got creative, saving time and money by sinking big wine barrels into the ground instead of hiring someone to build a lining. Eventually, though, these latrines would need to be emptied through the services of the *gongfermour* ('gong farmer'), who would clean out the privy for an understandably steep fee, or charge by the number of 'tuns' or barrels filled.

If you didn't have a home with a backyard privy, you could visit the public facilities. Funded by bequests made in generous people's wills, or by the city, the public latrines were accessible to everyone, and in some places even featured a tile floor (probably for ease of cleaning). These public restrooms were not a place for privacy, or separated by gender, but they were serviceable and available. Because these public latrines existed, medieval townsfolk had no patience for people who urinated or defecated in the street, although it did still happen on occasion, as it does today.

Monks knew the value of a decent latrine system, too. The ideal monastery outlined in the Plan of St Gall requires that there be enough privies for monks, guests, and servants' guests. This community of 300 monks, then, was meant to have eighty-three privies in total, all of which used water to flush away waste.

If you were lucky enough to live in a castle, you might have had your own ensuite garderobe within your chamber. This was basically a little closet of stone, inside which was a stone bench with a hole in it, preferably covered by a wooden slat or toilet seat for comfort. Many garderobes had little shelves on which a person could store the hay or linen scraps with which they needed to wipe – or on which they could set a candle – as well as a window for both light and ventilation. At least one Scottish castle's garderobe window is wider on the inside and narrower on the outside to prevent the person silhouetted on the privy at night from being shot.

Many posh castles, such as the White Tower in the Tower of London, even had one or two garderobes off the main hall for the convenience of those dining or meeting there. Unfortunately, even in the most luxurious of garderobes there were no sinks, though a person could use an ewer and basin on a table outside the door if the host was kind enough to provide them, and should the guest feel the need to wash afterwards.

The garderobes in castles tended to be built over the moat or outside the walls so that waste wouldn't be collected inside the walls. This was handy defensively, as besiegers who needed to cross a moat faced an ugly task, indeed. The downside, however, was that any hole outside the walls – even the most repulsive – was a vulnerability, as King John learned to his cost when French solders infiltrated Château Gaillard by climbing in through the hole in a garderobe. Talk about a dirty trick.

Because medieval Europeans simply did not have modern cleaning tools or products, it was impossible for both cities and people to be 'clean' by our standards. Still, we can see by the efforts they made and the time they spent on bathing, washing, and garbage removal that cleanliness and hygiene were important to them. The desire to look good, smell good, and have clean surroundings is well documented, and yet somehow, the medieval pursuit of good hygiene still remains a dirty little secret.

Chapter Two

Farming, Fasting, Feasting

For people who want to immerse themselves in the past, there's nothing quite like experiencing a medieval feast at one of the many themed restaurants across the world that offer both food and entertainment in a raucous, colourful setting. Eating simple food with the fingers, laughing and shouting at performers, and having your servants show you respect and deference as they deliver more food and drinks bring the medieval world closer, but how close?

What did people eat?

Most of the food medieval people ate was homegrown not too far from where they lived, so it consisted of local plants and livestock. Peasants worked on manorial farms to which they were legally tied as serfs, or which they rented from the lord as freemen. Not only did the farmers need to care for the crops they grew to feed themselves, but they also needed to work together to care for the lord's crops as part of their duty as vassals. This food could then be used to support the community in times of famine, feast, or siege.

Ploughing was done using teams of oxen, horses, and people, as extra hands were needed not only to guide the plough, but also to guide the animals. While the spread of a heavy, wheeled plough made things easier after the twelfth century, it was still a long process, and it involved everyone in the community. From planting, to ploughing, to watering, to weeding, to caring for animals; everyone from children to the elderly pitched in, and at harvest time, pitched in again to thresh, reap, and carry.

> The measurement of an 'acre' comes to us from Anglo-Saxon, and it means the amount of land that one team of oxen could plough in a day.

Grains made up a huge proportion of what people farmed and ate in the Middle Ages. People ate wheat, oats, and barley, turning all of the above into bread, pastry dough, porridge, and cakes. A catch-all meal was pottage: a grain of your choice mixed with leftover broth, meat, and whatever else was on hand, usually as a filling breakfast before heading out for the day.

Bread was a critical staple in medieval Europe. Monks, for example, each got a quarter of a four-pound loaf as their daily bread, and they even had special weights made to ensure everyone got their fair share. The vast majority of bread was black bread: a coarse, dense loaf that made up much of the overall medieval diet. In the mountainous areas of Italy, southern France, Spain, and Portugal, where it was difficult to grow grain, peasants even ate bread made out of chestnuts. White bread was known, but the fine white flour required meant it was reserved for the rich.

Grains of every type were ground into flour at water-powered mills whenever possible, usually owned by the local lord or monastery. People would deposit their sacks of grain and return later to pick up their flour. Because grit naturally sloughing off the millstone would often get mixed in with the flour (or because of unscrupulous millers who mixed sand into the flour to disguise their thieving) the near-constant consumption of bread caused significant wear and tear on medieval teeth, flattening the bumps out of their molars.

Other plants made up a large part of the medieval diet, too, including some we now think of as simply flavourful additions, such as leeks, onions, and garlic. Beans, lentils, and legumes supplied protein for diets lean on meat, while apples, pears, citrus fruits (depending on where you lived), and other plants supplied vitamins. Vegetables and herbs were grown in kitchen gardens both in the countryside and in the city.

Most medieval people, farmers and townsfolk, raised livestock of some kind, which allowed easy access to eggs and dairy products, including butter, milk and cheese. Without refrigeration, milk and butter were often seasonal products, while cheese lasted much longer. Bread and cheese made a nice, portable medieval lunch.

Because of religious restrictions, there were many days – including normal Fridays – on which the Christians who made up the majority of the population were not permitted to eat meat. On those days, fish was the main source of protein, sourced from both the sea and the plentiful rivers that crisscross Europe. As a result, fishing was a huge industry, and the location and use of fish traps enough of a nuisance that restrictions on using them in the Thames were written into that paragon of legal texts: Magna Carta. Some of the many types of fish that could be found on medieval plates were trout, salmon, herring, sole, mackerel, and pike.

Modern renditions of medieval feasts in books and on the silver screen always feature great amounts of meat, and this would certainly have been the case, depending on the wealth of the host. True medieval feasts would not have included giant turkey legs, however, as turkeys come from the Americas, which had not been 'discovered' yet (aside from a couple of abandoned Viking settlements). Incidentally, the same is true of tomatoes, potatoes, sweet corn, and chocolate.

Meat of all kinds was enjoyed whenever it was available, from familiar fare, such as beef, chicken, mutton, and pork; to game like venison, rabbit, boar, and squirrel; and finally, more unexpected meats, such as pigeon, lark, swan, and even peacock. As now, meat could be prepared in a huge variety of ways, from flavourful soups and stews, to juicy roasts, to the delicious meat pies and pasties that could be bought from a street vendor.

Didn't everyone just cook their meals at home?

Although every home would have had a place for a fire, whether in a central hearth or (later) a fireplace, some people had neither the space nor the equipment for a designated kitchen, depending on their means. For these people, anything more elaborate than the basic heating of a pot or roasting on a skewer would involve visiting a bakery or using communal ovens owned by the town, local lord, or nearby monastery. Even people with their own kitchens would make use of communal ovens, especially if they had a large number or variety of dishes to make. In Le Ménagier de Paris recipe for making Norse Pasties, he specifically notes that 'the pastry cook takes them uncooked to the baking shop'.

Monastic communities and castles, because they had many mouths to feed, usually had their own kitchens and bakeries, but even these would normally be separate from the main buildings because of the risk of fire. Baking involved superheating a small stone enclosure and then quickly removing the coals and putting in the dough or pastry. Roasting enough meat for a castle or group of monks and nuns involved massive fireplaces – often more than one. When you add the fires necessary for cooking sauces and savouries, the medieval kitchen becomes a very hot and hazardous place, indeed.

> Bread baked in medieval ovens got ashy on the bottom because it was placed directly on stone just heated by a fire. Because of this, the poshest medieval diners wouldn't have bothered with the lower crust, but rather the upper crust.

For people in cities, fast food was an option. Bakeries and street vendors offered bread, pies, and pasties for a quick lunch on the go, or roasted meat to take home. Taverns and inns offered hot food and tasty beverages. As now, these were more expensive options, but sometimes the only ones available to people who didn't have the time or resources to cook at home. In a time when no one had refrigerators, trips to the market were frequent, and fast food would have been a tempting option for impulse buys, just as it is today.

Wasn't the food all bland?

While it's true that eating the same food in different combinations based on what you have available can become tiresome, that doesn't mean that the food was bland. Peasants had most of the spices that are still regularly featured in modern spice racks available to them, such as the old favourites parsley, sage, rosemary, and thyme, as well as basil, oregano, garlic, and chives. Their inclusion in the thousands of modern recipes online goes to show that the possibilities for interesting dishes are endless using these flavours alone.

People with wealth could also buy spices from far afield, mixing them in combinations which may seem strange today, but are no less delicious for their unfamiliarity. Pepper, cinnamon, ginger, nutmeg, cumin, and cloves were common ingredients in recipe books, although their inclusion in books (expensive commodities, themselves) underlines their use in wealthier households, not peasant homes. Two oft-mentioned ingredients in medieval cooking are *poudre douce* and *poudre fort* ('sweet powder' and 'strong powder') and each of these was a combination of spices to be used together, much as we might list 'pumpkin spice' as just one ingredient in a modern recipe. The combinations varied, but *poudre douce* could contain spices such as might still be used in a pumpkin pie (cinnamon, cloves, ginger, sugar), while *poudre fort* would contain many of the same ingredients, with the addition of pepper. It's thanks to the long and complex trade routes that using shorthand like *poudre douce* in recipes was possible.

How far did the trade routes stretch?

Although it's common for people to think of medieval Europe as an isolated bubble (with the possible exception of the Holy Land) medieval trade routes were long enough that someone in Ireland could buy silk from China or spices and pigments from as far away as Africa or India. The cost of getting luxury items shipped that far was high, and therefore out of reach for those at the bottom of the social ladder, but the networks were definitely there for those who had both expensive and exotic tastes.

Coconut cups, and combs, boxes, and game pieces made of elephant ivory were likewise not strange to see in northern Europe, even in the Early Middle Ages. Other, more commonplace items like the alum required to set cloth dyes absolutely depended on these trade networks. Spices and silk were some of the most popular items brought westwards (there's a reason the major trade route through from Asia to

Europe is called the Silk Road), but technology and knowledge flowed both ways alongside luxury goods.

Did Europeans have a lot of contact with different cultures?

Yes. Medieval Europe was much more diverse than the Victorians who did much of the early scholarship on the Middle Ages assumed. A survey of manuscript images will show people with white skin, but also black and brown skin, curly hair, and turbans. Sometimes these figures are meant to be shown as enemies to white Europeans, but many times they are not. Because of the legacy of the Roman Empire, the continuing slave trade through the Early Middle Ages, and the intercontinental trade and pilgrimage routes, people in the big urban centres and port cities of Europe would not have been shocked to see a diverse range of faces.

When royals wed, they also tended to marry across borders in order to create, improve, or solidify relationships with other countries. Brides brought with them retainers from their homelands, who intermarried in their new homes. They also brought new trade relationships, which meant increased contact with the bride's home country and its culture.

When communities mixed in these and other ways, their cultures, fashions, entertainment, and food mixed, as well. Without travel and trade outside of their own borders, for example, Europeans would never have tasted sugar, showing that getting along with your neighbours can be sweetly rewarding, indeed.

What did people drink?

Some of the water in and around medieval cities would have been undrinkable, contaminated as it was by privies, animals, laundry, fulling, and tanning. The common idea that no one actually drank water, however, is a myth. Everywhere in medieval Europe, people sank wells to provide themselves with the water they needed for drinking, cooking, washing, and watering gardens. Cities provided central fountains and wells for their citizens, sometimes drawing water from sources outside of the city limits via lead pipes. In castles, especially, establishing a well was one of the first orders of business, as in times of siege the people trapped inside the castle's protective walls would die within days without a water source. Beyond wells and cisterns, people from the smallest homes to the largest castles channelled rainwater from their roofs into barrels.

In his *Canon of Medicine*, the eminent doctor Avicenna (the Anglicised name for Abū Alī al-Husain ibn Abdullāh ibn Sīnā) gave some good advice on which sources of water are best, and how to make it clean enough to drink. Water that is in continuous motion and exposed to the sun is better than standing water, he says, declaring (wisely) that the 'worst type is that transported in lead pipes.' In a passage straight out of a modern survival guide, Avicenna also notes, 'Water quality can be improved by boiling and distillation or by cooking it,' ('the best is distillation'). He suggests filtering the water, if possible, either by having it travel from one container to another via a 'wool wick'; by boiling it with wool and wringing the water out; or mixing it with burnt clay and then filtering it. Perhaps his most important tip on water, however, is that 'a filter must be used when drinking water [from an unknown source] to prevent leeches from being swallowed.'

The other beverage that just about everyone drank – even children – was ale. In the Middle Ages, domestic ale was truly domestic: rather than being made in a shop, it was most often made at home. Medieval women were the home brewers, creating batches of ale for their own households and selling the surplus at market for extra cash. Professional brewers who needed to create large supplies (for taverns and inns, for example) did tend to be men, as were most medieval professionals. For much of the period, people mainly drank ale, although in the late Middle Ages, beer – made with hops, that is – became popular across Europe, too.

Even monastic communities made and drank their own ale, and they also fermented honey from their beehives to create mead for drinking and for selling. Monastic orchards were a great place to find apples aplenty for making cider, and their carefully-tended vineyards supplied grapes for making wine.

Although grapes had been known to grow in England at some points during the Middle Ages, the best wines were made in southern Europe: France, Italy, Spain, and Portugal. Red wine was extremely popular, known even then to be amazing for your health, and it was drunk at all times of the day, although Avicenna sniffed, 'A smart person avoids drinking wine first thing in the morning.' Usually – and especially in the morning – wine was mixed with water to dilute the alcohol content.

Wine was especially popular among the upper classes, with good cellars being a sign of both prosperity and hospitality, two essential qualities for chivalrous lords and ladies. Not only were nobles drinking loads of wine, but they were also giving it away by the pitcher and the tun, sometimes as a way to pay loyal underlings like Geoffrey Chaucer. As the son of a wine merchant, himself, it's hard to say whether or not Chaucer – notorious for complaining of his poverty – would have been impressed by being paid in wine instead of cash.

Were they constantly drunk?

Luckily, people often drank what is known as 'small ale' which was lower in alcoholic content, and they did water their wine. That said, there was quite a lot of drunkenness overall, which seems to have been the cause of many a crime, according to the legal records of the time.

Drunkenness itself was considered to be sinful, as it was evidence of gluttony. One seventh-century source now called *Theodore's Penitential* – a book that outlined the correct way to atone for each sin – was especially concerned with vomiting from drunkenness, assigning thirty days of penance to monks, forty to 'a presbyter or deacon', fifteen for 'a lay Christian', and three for everyone else. If you were to vomit up your communion wafer, the penance would be seven days, unless you were legitimately sick (and not just drunk). Theodore does realise that sometimes drunkenness just happens, so he makes some considerate exceptions to these rules:

> If [the vomiting] is due to weakness or because [the drinker] has been a long time abstinent and is not accustomed to drink

or eat much; or if it is for gladness at Christmas or Easter or for any festival of a saint, and he then has imbibed no more than is commanded by his seniors, no offence is committed.

Considering the vast number of saints' days in the medieval calendar, it's not hard to imagine many a monk attempting to plead 'excessive gladness' in order to avoid doing penance.

Unfortunately for medieval Europeans, coffee was not available as a part of hangover cures, as it wasn't being drunk even in the Middle East until the fifteenth century, at which point it would start to make its way to Europe. The same goes for black tea. People did drink other teas – hot, herbal beverages that is – but not the familiar, blessedly-caffeinated varieties that modern people so love and crave, especially after a big night on the town.

Was everyone up for a night of drunken excitement?

No. For medieval Europeans, food and drink were a part of religious practice as well as just sustenance. Practicing Jews and Muslims followed the same guidelines for eating and drinking that are still used today, ensuring that their food was kosher or halal by trusting members of their own communities to prepare it appropriately. While medieval Christians didn't have religious rules around the preparation of their food, they were required to abstain from eating meat at certain times, as we saw earlier.

The monastic guidelines spelled out in *The Rule of St Benedict* are quite strict in terms of when, what, and how much monks were permitted to eat. St Benedict recommended two meals per day – one in the morning and one in the evening – with just two dishes served at each meal, and no one eating 'the meat of quadrupeds' unless it was critical to their recovery from illness. Children and the elderly were permitted to eat sooner if they needed to, however. In order to prevent 'grumbling or hardship', St Benedict allowed monks serving and doing the reading aloud during mealtimes to have extra bread and a drink an hour beforehand (they'd eat their full meal after everyone else), with the reader given watered wine right before he started.

> Because monks and nuns were not permitted to speak during meals, they came up with hand signs to indicate what they needed, such as shaking three fingers together to ask for salt.

Despite St Benedict's charity regarding these particular empty stomachs, fasting was a common part of life for the devoted part of the Christian majority. Beyond the rules for just avoiding meat on certain days, Christians were encouraged to fast at certain times of the year or as penance for sin, eating bread and water, or nothing at all.

In his rule, St Francis requires his monks to fast from All Saints Day (1 November) to Christmas, as well as every Friday, and throughout Lent if so desired. Advent and Lent are long stretches of time, so it's likely that Francis meant a severely restricted diet in these cases, such as the bread and water sometimes proscribed by penitentials. Because Franciscans were often mendicant friars – that is, they travelled to preach and convert – Francis allowed that 'it is lawful for them to eat all of the dishes which are placed before them.' No doubt there were some unpopular friars who made the most of this by dropping by people's houses right at dinnertime. Benedictines, who were not permitted to eat outside the monastery unless they were on a long trip, may have found themselves much more welcome.

What was a feast like?

The medieval feast was a grand spectacle, meant to feed and entertain hundreds of people at once. Feasts featured many courses from appetisers to desserts, each one of them meant to dazzle diners with both the generosity and wealth of the host.

The seating arrangements we often use for modern banquets – with a head table and other tables arranged in order of importance – follows medieval tradition. Typically, the host and hostess would sit at a head table on a raised platform, or dais, with the most important guests. All of these VIPs would sit on the same side of the table, facing the rest of the hall so everyone could see them. The rest of the guests would sit at long tables perpendicular to the head table, with the most important people closest to the head table, and everyone else seated in declining order of rank.

The tables used for meals in a great hall would typically be trestle tables; that is, they were long boards sitting on top of what resemble today's saw horses. Diners sat together on benches, although the elites at the head table may have had their own chairs, and even cushions. This arrangement made it easy to move the furniture when people weren't eating, allowing the great hall to fulfil its other functions throughout the day. Early medieval great halls featured a central fire with a hole in the roof to allow the smoke to escape, but as time went on, fireplaces were built, often behind the dais, and at intervals throughout the hall (depending on the wealth of the homeowner). If there was space available, room was left in the centre of the hall during the meal for entertainment. Many wealthy hosts also built musicians' galleries above their great halls so that guests could be entertained throughout the meal without the need to sacrifice floor space. The musicians' gallery was also a good place to situate the trumpeters required to play a fanfare to announce the entrance of important guests or each course as it arrived.

Usually, two diners shared the same plate or trencher. Trenchers were made of a slab of stale bread used as a plate, which was good for soaking up grease and sauce from the meal while also being economical. For a meal of forty people, Le Ménagier de Paris recommends buying '3 dozen brown trencher breads, half a foot long and 4 fingers wide and high, baked 4 days before' to give them the firm staleness they need. He also recommends assigning two servers 'who will cut the crust from the bread and make trenchers and saltcellars of bread' in preparation for the feast. They would be the ones to 'carry the salt and the bread [for eating] and the trenchers to the tables'.

It was considered extremely rude and uncouth to actually *eat* your trencher. Instead, you'd toss it into a scrap bucket carried through the hall by these servers at the end of the meal. Scraps could later be given to the dogs, the pigs, or the poor.

Did they really eat with their hands?

Yes they did, from the king all the way down to the lowest serf. Although each diner would have his or her own eating knife, carried on the belt, for carving or serving, people would not actually eat their food *off* their knives, unless they were extremely ill-mannered. Spoons were used at table for serving soups and sauces, and for eating. Forks, however, were not used in most of medieval Europe, with the exception of late medieval Italy and the Byzantine Empire. Most of Europe found forks to be strange and laughable even after the Middle Ages. Although they were used in the preparation of food, they were not used in the eating of it.

Beyond the famous Viking drinking horns, cups and goblets could be made of wood, pottery, leather, precious metals, or even blown glass. Like all of the other dishes at the table, cups and goblets ran the gamut from plain to elaborately carved, painted, glazed, or gilded. Diners shared their cups with their dining partners, just as they did their plates.

Unsurprisingly, the richer you were – or the richer you wished to appear – the richer your dishes. Instead of using bread trenchers, the rich could use plates made of gold or silver to accompany their gilded goblets and silver spoons. Some people intentionally invested in expensive dishes because they could be easily sold, traded, melted, or used as collateral if a quick cash injection was needed.

Because a feast was meant to feed the host's family, guests, tenants, and staff, while showing off his generosity and wealth, huge quantities of food were needed. Le Ménagier de Paris gives us an estimate:

> Monseigneur de Berry's people say that on Sundays and great feasts they need 3 beef cattle, 30 sheep, 160 dozen partridges, and as many rabbits as is necessary ... It is certainly so on great feasts and Sundays and Thursdays, but usually the other days it is 2 beef cattle and 20 sheep.

Le Ménagier also gives us an idea of what is needed to set the table for exalted guests, including tablecloths, cutlery, ewers, spice dishes, saltcellars, and 'decorative greenery'. In addition to the tablecloths, other linens were needed, including napkins, and towels for washing and drying the hands both before and after the meal.

Did people have any table manners?

Watching a modern movie set in the Middle Ages might lead a viewer to believe that there were no medieval table manners, but this is far from true. Not only were there rules about where and with whom a person could sit, but there were also many rules of etiquette to follow.

Because salt was an expensive commodity, sitting near the saltcellar was a sign of prestige. Important people sat 'above the salt' while less important people sat 'below the salt'. To further emphasise the status and wealth associated with salt, medieval saltcellars were some of the most elaborate and expensive dishes on the table. One saltcellar from thirteenth-century France is in the shape of a boat on a pedestal. It's made from gold and rock crystal, embellished with emeralds, pearls, and rubies. No wonder only the trustworthy were allowed to sit near it.

Sharing a trencher and cup meant that diners were given a close-up view of their partners' eating habits, and most medieval table manners address consideration for your companion. It was polite to give the best pieces of food from the serving tray to your companion, to ensure that you'd wiped your mouth before taking a sip from the shared cup, and to refrain from performing any personal grooming while at table.

A thirteenth-century poem lays out just a few of these important rules, some of which will sound extremely familiar to parents of small children:

> No-one should take food before the blessing has been made,
> Nor should he take a place other than that assigned to him
> by the one in charge of the meal.
> Refrain from eating until the dishes have been placed before you,

And let your fingers be clean, and your fingernails well-groomed.
Once a morsel has been touched, let it not be returned to the plate.
Do not touch your ears or nose with your bare hands.
Do not clean your teeth with a sharp iron while eating.
The salt is not to be touched with the food where it sits in the salt dish [i.e. no dipping].
If you can ... refrain from belching at the table.
Know that it is forbidden to put your elbow on the table.
It is ordered by regulation that you should not put a dish to your mouth [i.e. drink from your bowl].
He who wishes to drink must first finish what is in his mouth,
And let his lips be wiped first [with a napkin].
Nor can I avoid mentioning that he should not gnaw a bone with his teeth....
Once the table is cleared, wash your hands, and have a drink.

This last line sounds almost as if the diner was to reward himself for running a gauntlet, but table manners would have been second nature to medieval diners, just as they are to us.

Did they have dessert?

Yes. The relative rarity of sugar in medieval Europe didn't mean that people skipped dessert. Le Ménagier de Paris lists many delicious treats, such as gingerbread, candied orange peel, rose-sugar, and comfits. Pies, tarts, marzipan, and cookies moulded in the shape of biblical or mythological figures kept everyone happy, and were some of the most impressive foods to be found at a feast.

By far the most spectacular (food-related) aspect of medieval feasts would have been the *entremets* or *sotelties*, elaborate displays of culinary wizardry that signified the beginning of new courses. These were the moments in which a peacock or swan would be served fully (re)dressed in its own feathers, or a *cockatrice* – a dish with the front end of a chicken or capon stitched onto the hindquarters of a pig – would be presented with much fanfare. Although *entremets* were presented between (*entre*) courses, some of the most spectacular were reserved for the end of the meal.

Some of the *sotelties* that appeared to announce dessert were decidedly unsubtle, spectacular beyond belief. Because many of the plants used to make inks were edible, it meant that chefs could create masterpieces in full colour that complemented the theme of the feast, sometimes even giving them a shine with gold or silver foil. At one impressive early fifteenth-century wedding, each guest was treated to a personal pie decorated with his or her own heraldic device. Another wedding featured a jaw-dropping 'Castle of Love' with a wine fountain, several fully cooked and dressed animals (including a boar's head and a swan), and four live musicians, all integrated into a massive edible structure depicting a siege. Medieval *sotelties* were enough to put the most impressive modern reality contestants to shame.

These weddings weren't the only time delicious dishes were served to dazzle the eyes and ears along with the taste buds, either. Growing up, you may have heard the rhyme 'Sing a Song of Sixpence' which featured 'four and twenty blackbirds baked in a pie'. It may have sounded like nonsense that the birds miraculously begin to sing for the king when the pie was cut, but there were, indeed, many medieval feasts in which pie shells were baked and then filled with something amazing, such as birds or acrobats, who would burst out on cue to the delight of all.

Wasn't some of that a little unhygienic?

As we saw in Chapter One, medieval standards of hygiene were different from modern ones because germ theory hadn't yet been developed. Although there was an expectation of being clean when eating, and eating clean food, there was also a great reluctance to waste food that didn't need to be thrown away. Given how long and difficult the process was for getting any sort of food on the table, this makes sense.

While every effort would have been made to meet the hygienic standards of the time, like not having obvious dirt in the food, *Theodore's Penitential* has a few sections that make allowances for practices that wouldn't normally be encouraged. He says,

> He who eats unclean flesh or a carcass that has been torn by beasts shall do penance for forty days. But if the necessity of hunger requires it, there is no offense, since a permissible act is one thing and what necessity requires is another.

He makes similar exceptions for accidentally eating an unclean animal or eating food that has been accidentally touched by 'unwashed hands', by an animal, by blood 'or any unclean thing'.

If you did notice something contaminating your food, you could also follow Theodore's five-second rule:

> If a mouse falls into a liquid it shall be removed and sprinkled with holy water, and if it is alive it may be taken [for food]; but if it is dead, all the liquid shall be poured out and not given to man, and the vessel shall be cleansed.

If, out of necessity, you still have to use the liquid, that's okay, although not ideal. Not every case requires you to throw it out, though:

> If birds drop dung into any liquid, the dung shall be removed from it, and it shall be sanctified with [holy] water, and it shall be clean food.

Clearly, medieval food would not always have been up to modern health inspections, although it's just as clear that people did try to keep things clean.

As we've seen, medieval people (even peasants) had plenty of interesting varieties of food to eat, even if not all of it was available in the same places or at the same time. While a true medieval feast wouldn't have tasted much like the ones modern people continue to enjoy at dinner shows, the food would have been flavourful, plentiful, and interesting to the eye and the palate, with both table manners and tablecloths to go with it. For those who aren't interested in unfamiliar tastes, like peacock or cinnamon combined with pepper, perhaps the biggest takeaway is if you ever do time-travel back to the Middle Ages, bring a sandwich – and cover your cup.

Chapter Three

The Art of Love

If there's one thing medieval people loved even more than food, it was love. From tokens, to stories, to whole books of advice, Europeans were crazy about being crazy about each other.

Despite the common idea that medieval people were usually stuck in cold marriages having children whom they didn't allow themselves to love until they had passed the dangers of infancy, the truth is much more familiar. Some people married for love, while others married for security; some people deeply adored their children, while others didn't have much to do with theirs; some people had affairs outside of their marriages, while other people only dreamt about it; some people were married for decades and mourned their spouses forever, while others stayed together for decades just because it made financial sense. Love was as wonderful and painful and magical and heart-breaking as it is today.

Did medieval people date?

Yes, although not so privately as we do today. Couples went on outings together in public spaces where they could remain under the watchful gaze of their guardians. Young love and lust were something for families to keep an eye on, as there were lots of opportunities for people to fall for each other, for better and for worse. Many (if not most) tradesmen would have had teenage apprentices living with them in close proximity to their daughters, while teenage girls often took up positions as household servants before marriage, bringing them into close contact with the family for whom they worked. Even in rural areas, teens were a good pair of extra hands to have around, so young men and women would've been back and forth to each other's farms on a regular basis. Proximity has always been a key factor in romance, so it wouldn't be surprising if a medieval teenager's first crush was someone he or she was thrown together with in a living and working situation.

For nobles, who traditionally had their sons raised in other aristocratic households from about age 7 or 8 for the sake of their knightly training, the young squire in the house might be equally as distracting to – or distracted by – their daughters. This could be a good thing if the parents were already interested in a marriage alliance between the two families, since it gave the young people a chance to get to know each other in relatively neutral conditions. On the other hand, it could actively create problems for those who had betrothed their children elsewhere if love developed between the wrong pairs.

Being in the marriage market, as we know, isn't exclusive to young people, and plenty of widows and widowers were also looking to find love, security, companionship, or compatibility. There were many places for medieval singles to mingle, including the marketplace, church, festivals, and – for those who were rich enough – in hunting parties. Tournaments, during which love was praised and celebrated, were another place where people of all ranks could meet their peers and flirt. All of these places gave people opportunities in which they might have a little more freedom to speak, while still being respectably visible.

If a couple took a shine to each other, they could exchange love tokens and gifts as a sign of affection, or as a promise to marry. In *The Art of Courtly Love*, Andreas Capellanus ('Andreas the chaplain') reports,

> A woman who loves may freely accept from her lover the following: a handkerchief, a fillet for the hair, a wreath of gold or silver, a breastpin, a mirror, a girdle, a purse, a tassel, a comb, sleeves, gloves, a ring, a compact, a picture, a wash basin, little dishes, trays, a flag as a souvenir [or] any little gift which may be useful for the care of the person or pleasing to look at or which may call the lover to her mind, if it is clear that in accepting the gift she is free from all avarice.

Archaeological discoveries have confirmed that these gifts were indeed often exchanged in the name of love, especially mirrors, combs, brooches, and rings made of gold, bone, or glass. One of the most unusual and touching finds was a spur found on the battlefield at Towton, engraved with the words 'in loyal love all my heart'.

Weren't all of the marriages arranged?

No. While it was rare for people to marry without the approval of their parents, just as it is today, not every marriage was prearranged, and the bride and groom usually got to have their say even if it was. Technically, a medieval marriage was not valid without the consent of both parties, so although coercion was not unheard of, evidence of coercion meant that the marriage could be contested even if it was consummated. Although medieval marriage was about more than love (namely property, social standing, legitimacy, and honour), allowing your children to marry someone they loved – or at least liked – saved everyone both heartaches and headaches.

Most common people didn't get married until they were in their late teens or early twenties since, by then, they had finished their apprenticeships or their contracts as household servants and had saved up enough money to establish their own households. By that point, people had met quite a lot of potential spouses, and they and their families had figured out who might be the best match.

The church had strict laws forbidding people who were too closely related by blood (consanguinity) to marry, something that caused never-ending headaches for aristocratic matchmakers, whose political matches often required a dispensation from the pope to get around these rules. People of the lower classes weren't restricted by necessity to such a small pool of potential spouses, and they married into families from their own villages as well as from others within the parish who they may have come into contact with at common markets and fairs, through trade partnerships, or through friends of friends.

The political alliances conducted through marriage meant that royal and noble children were often betrothed – or even married –

before they'd reached adulthood. In these cases, or in ones in which the couple lived too far apart at the time of the ceremony, a proxy stood in their place to speak the vows. Even if children were technically married, there was no expectation of sexual intercourse before they were older. Unfortunately, there are some cases in which children were married to adults who didn't wait until they were fully grown to have sex. One of these was Margaret Beaufort, who gave birth to the future Henry VII (Henry Tudor) at the age of 13 or 14, an event that seems to have been physically traumatic enough that she was no longer able to have children. Many people strongly disapproved of this, however.

Though the vast majority of aristocratic marriages were arranged, even nobles sometimes got the chance to marry the person of their choice. Edward, the Black Prince of England and heir to the throne, waited until he was in his thirties to marry, choosing someone entirely inappropriate, not to mention within the restricted degrees of consanguinity: his second cousin Joan, the Fair Maid of Kent. His furious father, Edward III, had to quickly write to the Pope and get a dispensation, which was granted, and then hold a more formal ceremony for the couple.

A common impression of medieval marriage is that it was grim and dismal, and though there were definitely some unhappy marriages (just like today), even arranged marriage could turn out to be happy for both spouses, who turned to each other in sickness and in health, for richer and for poorer, as partners both inside and outside of the bedroom, and discovered that time and a life built together had inspired mutual affection and real love.

How did they get married?

Getting married in the Middle Ages was almost too simple. All the couple had to do was to speak their intention to marry and then have sex, and they were married. Even if they said they'd be married someday and under some conditions, having sex *at any time afterwards* made the marriage legally binding, whether or not the conditions were met.

A spouse could later contest that the marriage should be annulled on the grounds that preconditions were not satisfied, but until the annulment was granted, the couple was married. No priest, no church, no rings, no paper contracts, no witnesses necessary.

As you might imagine, this was a legal nightmare. People could be legitimately confused about whether or not they were married and could easily be married to more than one person at a time. To sort this out, at the Fourth Lateran Council in 1215, Pope Innocent III tightened up the rules on marriage, requiring the banns to be read out in church well before the marriage, so that anyone who might be married to the bride or groom already (or think they might be, or know someone who might be) could speak up before everyone imperilled their souls through bigamy. Even with all these new conditions, all that was actually required was consent and consummation for a marriage to be legally binding. Still, people increasingly preferred to get married within churches instead of on the church porch, as they previously had tended to do, with the blessing of a priest.

Brides didn't wear white in the Middle Ages, but rather the best clothes they had, as did everyone else. Often brides would wear a new girdle, given to them by their grooms during a formal betrothal or handfasting ceremony. One early fifteenth-century girdle discovered in London may have been such a bridal gift. It was decorated with the words '*tout monn coer*': 'all my heart'.

During the ceremony, the priest blessed the couple and their rings (if they could afford them), and the couple promised in front of the gathered witnesses that they would take each other as husband and wife. With the exchange of rings and vows, the bride and groom were married. After the ceremony was a good dinner – a feast if it could be afforded – and dancing, just like today.

Royal weddings, of course, were epic, with celebrations going on throughout the day, throughout the capital city. Tournaments and feasts, entertainment and dancing could last well beyond the wedding day, too. Princesses who married kings were celebrated twice: once for their weddings and once again for their queenly coronations.

What about the wedding night?

Most couples would not have been totally ignorant of what was about to happen on their wedding nights. For one thing, most couples who were not aristocrats were marrying in their late teens or twenties, so they were old enough to have been part of adult conversations for quite some time, if they hadn't already had sex, themselves. Also, everyone was well-acquainted with the habits of the animals which were ubiquitous in the countryside, as well as in towns. On top of that, medieval humour was extremely ribald, with dirty jokes being part of festivals, fabliaux, songs, and even religious plays. Finally, especially in rural communities, the lack of personal space within a home would've made it difficult not to witness some sort of sexual activity, even between the most discreet parents.

For a couple to be unquestionably, legally, married, it was necessary for them to have sex, so it was easier for everyone if that particular item on the list was checked off on the wedding night, if possible. Ideally, both parties would be virgins, although this is not likely to have been the case for everyone. The bride, especially, was meant to be a virgin, as evidence of her having sex before marriage might cast doubt on the parentage of any children who were born in the first nine months. However, not everyone went around waving bloody sheets the morning after. People without property, lineage, or power invested in the couple's union didn't necessarily care one way or the other if the bride was a virgin, and anyway, there was a strong possibility that she might have already had sex before marriage – with the groom, himself.

What about their sex lives?

The church's take on marriage was that people should not have sex at all unless they're planning to have children, so if you were going to have sex, it had to be within marriage. The go-to phrase, courtesy of St Paul, was that it was 'better to marry than to burn', which really sells it.

According to the church and the law, each partner owed the other a conjugal or marital debt; that is, they had to provide sex whenever their spouse wanted it. Although we may assume that it was always the wife having to sleep with her husband whether she wanted to or not, legally it went both ways. If a woman's husband was impotent, it was grounds for an annulment of the marriage, as he would not be able to give her children. In one particularly notorious case, prostitutes were brought in to see if the man in question really was impotent. After the prostitutes had unsuccessfully plied their trade, they scolded the poor man for marrying a woman when it wasn't possible for him to get her pregnant, or 'please her better than that'.

In fact, medieval cultural beliefs were just the opposite of modern Western ones: women – especially married women – were thought to be lustier than men, and it was understood that they'd find pleasure in sex just as men did. In one French *fabliau*, a woman confesses her sexual sins to her husband who is disguised as a priest:

> It would be difficult to find
> even one woman who's inclined
> or even capable to husband
> her lust, however fine her husband.
> Because our nature drives us to it,
> we can't resist it, and we do it,
> and those we marry are too dense,
> too harsh, and too vindictive, hence
> we daren't disclose ourselves to them
> or speak our needs regarding men,
> for they would think that we are tarts
> if we admitted that our hearts
> had such needs, so we have no choice
> but to rely on serving boys.

In aristocratic marriages, especially, it was very possible that you'd be married to someone who you didn't particularly like – in or out of the bedroom – but the church was adamant: adultery was not to be tolerated. Adulterers were shamed, fined, or shunned by the community at best, and punished by being stripped, beaten, and run out of town, or killed by a spouse at worst (although this was illegal). Of course, the vast majority of punishments for adultery were doled out to women, possibly because pregnancies betrayed them. For men, there was a certain amount of 'boys will be boys' acceptance around adultery among the elites and the royals. This double-standard was as ironic as it was destructive, given that it was women who were 'known' to be lustier than men.

Just because people couldn't commit adultery, however, didn't mean they couldn't dream about it. Many of the most famous romances circled around themes of adulterous love, especially following the twelfth century. The love triangle between King Arthur, Queen Guinevere, and Sir Lancelot is probably the most famous example of an adulterous love that is at once so romantic and so powerful that the lovers risk the highest form of treason in medieval society. But while courtly lords and ladies played at adultery, and even turned a blind eye to some of it, an open relationship with someone who was not your spouse was not acceptable unless you were beyond reproach, like royalty, and only if you were male.

What about LGBTQIA+ people?

Unfortunately, deviance from the plain vanilla type of sexual relationship was not acceptable under any circumstances during the Middle Ages. In monotheistic Europe, there was no tolerance for even the casual kind of same-sex relationships that had been previously accepted in some situations (such as those between Greek and Roman soldiers on campaign). Open love and marriage were not even a distant possibility.

It's important to note that sexual preference, unlike gender, was not considered to be static in the Middle Ages. That is, while people were considered either men or women (with no fluidity), no one was seen as categorically 'gay' or 'straight' because medieval people did not think of these as distinct categories. Instead of being concerned with sexual identities, medieval people focused on categorising the actual sexual acts as either acceptable or unacceptable, whether or not they happened once or habitually, and whether or not they were performed between women and men, men and men, or women and women. Sodomy – the label medieval people used for a range of what were considered 'deviant' sexual acts, especially anal sex – was a grievous sin, whether it was between men, or between a man and a woman. Anal sex was considered worse between men because it upset the gender binary, too: one partner was a man in a 'woman's role'.

Everyone was expected to have carnal desires, just as everyone was expected to abstain from all sex except for married sex for the express purpose of having children. Desiring someone of the same gender was a sin, but then so was adulterous desire (although, admittedly, it was considered much less of one). Keeping desires within the walls of one's own mind without acting on them, and asking God's forgiveness for lusty or deviant thoughts, was the ultimate goal for all medieval Christians.

Since asexuality was considered the height of Christian morality during the Middle Ages, asexual people could be comfortable as members of religious houses, where not only would there be no official expectation to have sex, but their abstinence would be considered both admirable and praiseworthy. In broader society, however, men and women were continually pressured to marry and have children (much like today). Some people did manage to opt out of conjugal relations for religious reasons, with the permission of their spouses, but this was not something a person could count on.

Cloistered communities were meant to be completely celibate; however, the fact that monks and nuns were sometimes having sex with each other was an open secret to the point at which people made homophobic jokes about it, much as people today will joke about same-sex relationships – and abuse – in modern prisons. In the same way, these jokes were meant to be titillating and to generate disgust, not acceptance.

Among the series of charges brought against the Templars, a military order which followed rules similar to monastic ones, was the accusation that they were sodomites; that is, that they had sex with each other. While this was likely a cheap shot that King Philip the Fair figured (correctly) would turn people against them, the Templars themselves had tightened their rules to explicitly remind the brothers that they were absolutely not allowed to have sexual contact with each other on pain of expulsion from the order. This is a much clearer indication that there were at least some Templars falling in love with each other (or having dangerous flings).

Though behaviour outside of heterosexual, gendered norms was condemned and punished, people were not immediately sentenced to death for their transgressions. Most often, a person would be punished and released, just as heretics were. It was committing the same acts more than once despite this 'correction' that led to harsher punishments and executions.

In *Theodore's Penitential*, the penance meted out for 'he who after his twentieth year defiles himself with a male' was fifteen years, although this seems to imply habitually, as Theodore's rules go on to say that 'he who commits this sexual offence once shall do penance for four years'. The nature of the man as an adult also seems to be significant, as a boy is given penance of 'two years for the first offence; if he repeats it, four years.' Surprisingly, it is oral sex between men – not anal sex – that was considered by Theodore to be 'the worst of evils'. Unsurprisingly, the penance for women was much lower: three years for either sex with a woman or 'solitary vice'.

Some people were known to have dressed as members of the opposite gender, but it's unclear from the sources whether those people were motivated by a need or desire to live as a member of the other gender, or for another purpose. Katherina Hetzeldorfer was perhaps what we might now call transgender, purposefully living in the world as a man. Two prostitutes, Ronaldino/Ronaldina Ronchaia in Venice and John/Eleanor Rykener in London, dressed as women when they solicited sex from men, but it's difficult to know how these two perceived themselves; Ronchaia was in a sexless marriage, and while Rykener had sex with men in the dress of a woman, he also had sex with women as a man (seemingly not as a prostitute). Rykener did take on other work in his female identity, but the closest he gets to stating a sexual preference is to quip that he prefers priests because he gets more money out of them. Joan of Arc wore men's clothing for what seem to have been practical purposes; nonetheless, her 'relapse' into wearing them instead of women's clothing was cited by her judges as a major reason for her execution. Hetzeldorfer was also executed, drowned in the Rhine, while her sexual partners, who had always presented as female both in their dress and in their passive role in the bedroom, were given the lesser punishment of exile.

With all this talk of condemnation and punishment, it's easy to lose sight of the loving relationships that did exist, even if their traces are faint. It was not unusual in the Middle Ages for people to have close, passionate relationships with members of the same sex, even if they were unconsummated. People might have raised eyebrows, but without the proof of sexual acts, how could anyone say for sure that these relationships weren't just intense friendships? The discretion that may have saved the lives of many LBGTQIA+ people at the time is precisely what makes tracing their relationships so difficult.

One particularly touching memorial that might well be of a same-sex couple in a long-term relationship is that of two knights buried together in the late fourteenth century. Their tomb records that they had been by each other's side for thirteen years, and in a story reminiscent of many long-term loving couples, when one died, the other died just days later. The end of their story, though, is both unusual and sweet: like a married couple, the two were buried with their coats of arms joined together on their shields.

Even priests were having sex?

Yes. The sex lives of clergy were a constant source of amusement and ridicule, beyond just homophobic wisecracks. Part of this was because not all clergy were celibate (some were married), part of this was because celibacy was a struggle for others, and part of this was because medieval people just loved dirty jokes, and celibacy was an easy target.

During the Early Middle Ages, many members of the clergy were married, since ideas about celibacy had not been widely enforced. When Innocent III introduced his reforms at the Fourth Lateran

Council, he declared that none should be married from now on – common law or otherwise. Priests didn't always listen, even to the venerable pope, and many still lived with women, sometimes under the guise of 'housekeepers', even as they bore the priests' children (presumably, they stared the community down and dared them to say anything).

Other men of the cloth, especially young men studying to be clerks, were the constant butt of jokes about seducing young women, especially in fabliaux. Fictitious friars were also frequently having affairs with married women and hiding from their husbands.

Even nuns were not free of suspicion, as they required a priest to perform mass for them and to hear their confessions. This meant the regular visitation of a man within the cloister walls, a tempting opportunity for sexual dalliance for priests and nuns who were all-too casual with their vows. Some ordinances for nuns prohibit the sisters from being in the orchards at night, in case they planned to meet lovers there. It's quite likely that these situations did occur from time to time, although not to the extent that medieval jokes imply.

While most medieval jabs were meant to point out or poke fun at consensual relationships, some priests – and nuns within their own communities – actually did abuse their positions for sexual purposes. In Montaillou, France, an inquiry was made into the activities of a local priest who used the intimacy of confession as a way of instigating sexual relationships. One of the women testified that the priest would make her wear an amulet around her neck every time they had sex. This may have been a contraceptive – a pessary – meant to keep the priest's activities relatively secret. Fortunately, he was caught anyway.

People were using contraceptives?

Believe it or not, people have been using contraceptives since ancient times, and it's likely that some of them worked – at least to a point.

The most common form of contraception that women could, and did, use was breastfeeding. As long as they were nursing, it was difficult for them to conceive. Of course, people anxious (or pressured) to have more children, such as queens and other aristocrats, gave the feeding of their children into the care of a wet nurse, which meant that this simple form of birth control wasn't possible for them.

Another common form preventing pregnancy was simple *coitus interruptus*, or 'pulling out' as it tends to be called today. This is not always effective at the best of times, although it was better than nothing at all. We know from the penance they got for doing it that some people were also having sex *in femoribus* (between the legs) so this could also have been an option used to avoid pregnancy.

Alternatively, or in addition to these methods, women also used herbal remedies to keep from becoming pregnant. Preventing a pregnancy was against the church's teaching, and aborting one was even more serious, so it's not surprising that most of our information about the methods used is found in treatises denouncing these practices. In fact, one of the ways we know about medieval contraception at all is that priests were meant to ask in confession, 'Have you drunk any *malificium*, that is herbs or other agents, so that you could not have children?'

Many of the herbs that could be used for contraception had unsubtle names, such as artemisia (named after the virgin goddess), myrrh (named after a tragic Greek legend of incest), rue, and birthwort. Other common plants, such as willow, dittany, juniper, pennyroyal, and Queen Anne's lace would have worked, too. These plants have been known since antiquity to prevent conception, so it's extremely likely that they were known in the Middle Ages, as well. Just how well known is a mystery. Doubtless, women passed on this information about preventing pregnancy orally, just as they would have passed on information about pregnancy and birth, which leaves us with only the barest traces in the written record.

Did they love their children?

This is a very common question to which there is an intuitive answer: yes, medieval people absolutely loved their children. While the way they raised them may seem strange and unfamiliar to us, the care with which parents provided their children with toys and food, and the grief they felt when they lost them, are both familiar and clear.

Babies were usually born at home in the company of female family members and midwives. Medieval hospitals did occasionally have maternity wards, funded through private donations to provide care for poor and/or unmarried mothers. Other hospitals specifically refused to help pregnant mothers because of the sin writ large on their bodies.

Prayers, amulets, and charms were used to help keep the mothers safe from harm during childbirth, and attendants sometimes wrapped elaborate birth girdles – long scrolls with prayers and religious images written on them – around their stomachs as added protection. Invocation of the saints, including the Virgin Mary, Mary's mother St Anne, and St Margaret were spoken as additional forms of protection.

> St Margaret was the patron saint of pregnant women, since, by invoking the name of Jesus, she had burst forth unharmed from the stomach of a dragon who had devoured her.

Labour was the most dangerous time for women, with both mother and baby at risk of dying from complicated deliveries. Forceps had not yet been invented, but midwives could do their best to gently turn and ease babies through the birth canal with hands liberally slathered with butter, coconut oil, or a 'decoction of linseed and fenugreek', as *The Trotula* advises. Although medieval people did have painkillers, these were not generally used in childbirth, especially since the pain of labour was meant to be felt by women as penance for Eve's sin.

For mothers and babies in distress, caesarean sections could be performed as an absolute last resort. At a time before modern antibiotics it was very likely that a woman could die from this surgery, so it was only undertaken if it looked as though the mother would likely die anyway (or had, in fact, just died).

Babies were baptised within a day or two of birth, as church dogma decreed that unbaptised babies ended up in hell because of the original sin they carried. As a prime example of how much people actually did care about children, however, the church permitted anyone at the birth to baptise a baby in distress if a priest was not present, so that the baby would not be denied heaven on a technicality. Usually, this hasty baptism would have been performed by the midwife, but parents could also perform the baptism just by pouring water over the baby's head and declaring that the child was being baptised in the name of the Father, Son, and Holy Spirit.

Mothers were considered to be rendered impure through childbirth and they were not meant to resume normal life as part of the community until they had been 'churched' or purified by a ceremony forty days after the birth. During this time, mothers would be visited and supported by the women of the community. As not everyone had the luxury of such care and support, it's difficult to know how closely ordinary women kept to this in reality.

Peasant women would keep their babies with them, close by as they went about their daily work, or watched by siblings. The good news was that mothers and babies could stay together, although the bad news (as anyone who's had a baby of their own can attest) was that peasant parents still had to go about their work while weary and sleep-deprived.

Aristocratic women, especially queens, were not always able to spend much time with their infants, as it was thought to be more correct for babies to be in the care of nannies or nurses. Some royal children had their own households, completely separate from their parents, who would visit only when their schedules allowed. This meant that the royal parents got a bit more sleep, but that their relationships with their children weren't always especially close.

What was childhood like?

Although in the past, people have thought that medieval children were simply treated as tiny adults, in reality, medieval childhood was not just a time for work, but for learning, and for play. Medieval children were interested in the same sorts of things that modern children are interested in: songs, games, sports, and make-believe. Archaeological digs across Europe have unearthed dolls, tiny horses, toy soldiers, and even miniature pots and pans. In an adorable personal anecdote, the twelfth-century cleric and historian Gerald of Wales recalls his brothers making sandcastles as children, while he made sand monasteries.

While they had some freedom to play, children were also expected to help out around the house with chores, even ones that we might now consider too difficult for children. They were responsible for cooking, carrying loads, caring for animals, as well as learning skills they would need in later professions. Tiny thimbles found in England and children's fingerprints pressed into German clay pots and tiles suggest that children helped their parents with work beyond just domestic chores.

If time could be spared, children of both genders learned how to read (even if they never learned how to write), and their first teachers were usually their mothers. The connection between mothers, children, and reading is strong enough that pictures of the Virgin Mary often show her with an open book and Jesus on her lap. Mary's mother, St Anne, is likewise often depicted holding a book, presumably the one from which she taught Mary. These images, not surprisingly, are often featured in prayer books for women.

Unless they were educated at a convent in preparation for a life as a nun, girls learned how to run the home, including who was in charge of which duties, what supplies were needed, and how to work with staff to keep things going. This wasn't just for show: medieval women, unlike some of their other historical female counterparts, were expected to pick up where their husbands left off if they went to war, away on business, or died, and these women did so with competence, either in the name of their husbands, or in their own right.

Boys who were preparing to enter the church went to cathedral schools or monasteries and learned to master seven subjects, categorised into the *trivium* and the *quadrivium*. The *trivium* consisted of (Latin) grammar, rhetoric, and logic and the *quadrivium* of arithmetic, geometry, astronomy, and music. Some of the books that have proven to be Rosetta Stones for our modern understanding of dead languages such as Anglo-Saxon are school books meant to teach boys Latin. School could be hard in that corporal punishment was considered an acceptable way to correct mistakes, but literacy could take children far in life. Gifted students or those dedicated to a life in the church could go on to university and advanced training as teachers, lawyers, and doctors, or they could pursue careers in royal service or the church.

Aristocratic boys who were not given to the church were, of course, trained in combat and horsemanship. Using wooden swords, bows, and lances, they worked until they became proficient enough to become squires for older knights. In their mid-to-late teens, squires could become knights if they proved themselves sufficiently worthy in feats of arms, or in order to take their place as lords. Aristocratic boys were still given a formal education alongside their martial one, learning to read and write, as well as to care for their lands and tenants.

Did everyone die young?

The average medieval person lived only until his or her mid-forties, but this doesn't mean that no one grew old. People worked until they were no longer able to, at which point they reduced their workloads, found jobs suitable to their new stage in life, or relied on the support of the community. Plenty of the tasks required to keep a household functioning – from gardening, to cooking, to caring for children – could be performed by people who were no longer able to guide a plough or pull a cart. Older matrons could provide services as midwives or nurses, and women over 50 were considered to be the ideal laundresses in some religious communities, unflatteringly because they were considered to be less tempting to the priests and monks (and past the age of troublesome pregnancies). Guilds collected money from their members as a sort of pension to prevent elder guildsmen from being impoverished. For those who did fall into poverty, almshouses and hospitals were places where elders could receive care if they had no family members to help them.

More often than not women outlived their husbands and the majority of them, given the choice, decided not to remarry. This was likely because a widow could control property in her own right while, in some parts of Europe, a wife could not. Widows were more than capable of using a lifetime's worth of skills and experience to keep themselves and their households afloat. Those who needed extra income and didn't want to become midwives or nurses could pick up piecework in the textile industry as they might have done throughout their marriages, or put their brewing skills to good use.

How did people cope with death?

It was not at all rare for medieval people to lose family members at any stage of life. Along with the normal risks of disease and accident, infant mortality was especially high, women frequently died in childbirth, and men were killed in wars. The sheer frequency of death, especially of babies, has led people in the centuries since the Middle Ages to speculate that medieval people did not get that upset by it. This, of course, is nonsense. Evidence of medieval grief abounds in the tributes paid to lost loved ones in statuary, tombs, and the written word.

Times of grief were some of the most dangerous times for medieval Christians, as these were the moments in which the bereaved truly began to question God's plan, and even his existence. It is no coincidence that criticism of the church and its clergy was never higher than it was after the Black Death, when up to 60 per cent of Europe's population had been wiped out. Christine de Pizan, said to be the first professional female writer, had a husband who died of illness far from her. She writes of being driven by grief almost to the point of endangering her immortal soul:

> I can never forget this great,
> incomparable suffering, which brings my
> heart to such torment, which puts into my
> head such grievous despair, which
> counsels me to kill myself and break my
> heart.

On the other hand, moments of bereavement also had the potential to bring people more closely into their faith. One of the most beautiful poems in Middle English, *Pearl*, was written by a father who had lost his 1-year-old daughter. She was his pearl, and falling asleep at her graveside, he dreams about her showing him the delights of heaven which she now enjoys.

What actually happened when someone died?

If at all possible, in the moments before a person died, the local priest would be sent for to perform the last rites. People were terrified of dying unshriven, so there are often accounts of priests hearing the confessions of people who didn't actually end up dying after all. During the Black Death, when mortality rates overwhelmed the number of priests available, the church allowed for anyone at the bedside to absolve the dying, giving them a chance to reach heaven. People about to enter a battle often chose to be shriven, although there was always the risk of sinning – such as swearing – between the soldier's confession and his death.

Once a person had died, his or her body was washed, wrapped in a shroud, processed to the church, and prepared for funeral. Candles would be placed around the body to burn all night, and a mass would be said in the morning before the body was taken to the graveyard outside the church. Bells were rung out before the mass and as the body was brought to its grave, and the deceased's best robe would be given to the church as payment.

Royals, of course, had different rules in that they had larger funerary processions, often with wooden effigies on top of the casket, and elaborate tombs. Occasionally, they even had their hearts buried in separate locations from their bodies, although the church did not approve of this in general.

> Edward III's wooden funerary mask survives, and shows a slight droop to his mouth, leading some historians to speculate that the slow mental deterioration of his last few years of life may have been due to a series of strokes.

Aristocrats, high-ranking ecclesiastics, and the very rich had tombs within the church. If people didn't want, or couldn't afford, fancy tombs, they could be memorialised with an engraved slab integrated into the church floor or on its walls. Many of these tombs and slabs are still visible in European churches.

A distinctly medieval tradition that grew in popularity after the Black Death was the creation of 'cadaver tombs'. These showed the deceased in a state of decay, being eaten by worms, snakes, and toads; or as a skeleton, either with an effigy of the person as they were in life, or without. These tombs were meant to be gruesome and shocking, a visible counter to the beautiful effigies and tombs elsewhere in the churches. Their purpose was to remind the living of the fragility and transience of life, and that eventually death comes for us all. They were a visual warning to repent of sin before it was too late, as death can come at any moment, whether your soul is prepared or not. Cadaver tombs were a part of the *memento mori* ('remember death') movement in late medieval art and song. It isn't unusual to find dancing skeletons as part of funerary monuments or in church murals.

People were buried in coffins whenever possible, their shrouds if a coffin was not affordable. Because church graveyards had a limited amount of space (especially in cities), graves were used more than once. Epidemics and battles sometimes saw the use of burial pits, but a proper Christian burial was important to ensure heaven was attained, so these were rare cases.

Not everyone was permitted to be buried within the churchyard, however. People who had not been baptised, who had been excommunicated, or had committed suicide were not allowed to be buried in consecrated ground. Suicides were sometimes buried at crossroads, especially in late medieval Germany and England. These burials were meant to be humiliating to the deceased, warning others against committing this sin.

Because unbaptised babies were technically not Christians, church doctrine decreed that they were consigned to hell, even if they were stillborn or murdered. Sympathetic clergy tried to soften the blow by suggesting that these children were baptised 'by the Holy Spirit' or by an angel. Others scolded midwives for pretending stillborns were alive long enough to baptise them, thereby allowing the parents to give the babies a

Christian burial. In a heart-breaking case which demonstrates the depth of the grief and love of medieval parents, Hereford Cathedral was given permission in the fourteenth century to fence off and lock its graveyard at night, as bereaved parents – at the peril of their own souls – were secretly burying their unbaptised children in the consecrated ground of the churchyard, desperate to give them a chance at reaching heaven.

Even for the baptised, there was anxiety around who would be allowed into heaven and who would not. One fifteenth-century Valencian poet, Ausiàs March, was tormented by the fact that he did not know where his beloved's soul had gone. Worse, he was concerned that he may have inadvertently contributed to her sins and therefore risked her place in the afterlife. He writes,

> In vain I clench my hands in prayer: all that
> could happen has already come to pass.
> If in Heaven, joy ineffable is hers;
> if she's in Hell, then foolish are my prayers.
> If that's the case, annihilate my soul,
> and turn my being back to nothingness,
> especially if because of me she's damned;
> with suffering so cruel do not afflict me.

Elsewhere, March speaks to the anxiety of all bereaved medieval Christians more plainly: 'If I could be sure she with the blessed dwells, I would not wish that she were still alive.'

The church refined the idea of purgatory in the thirteenth century as the sort of middle ground for people who were essentially good, but who, through circumstance, might otherwise be consigned to hell after death. People's sins were purged here over time, cleansing their souls enough that eventually they could ascend to heaven. Given human nature, it's not surprising that many people suspected that they might end up in purgatory atoning for sins they didn't confess, didn't remember, or had thought were too minor to bother with. In order to mitigate this, people gave offerings to the church so that the more spiritual members of the community could pray for them and ask God to forgive their sins. Loved ones could also pay a church or monastery to say masses for the deceased, or to pray for their souls for a certain length of time. The wealthy went a step further and established churches, monasteries, and convents in the name of their loved ones, ensuring the gratitude of the community, both within and without the walls, and the remembrance of the departed in daily prayers.

The fact that there were so many avenues for bereaved people to aid their beloved spouses, family members, and friends after death shows just how much love there was between people in life, and that the normalcy of death didn't diminish the impact it had on the bereaved. Although they may have hoped and trusted that they'd be together in the afterlife, many people stayed as close to each other as they could on Earth, regardless, being buried beside the ones they loved, their effigies even sometimes holding hands.

While it's true that the relationships people had with each other in medieval Europe were frequently shortened by death, they loved each other intensely despite the risk. Love tokens, letters, poetry, and memorials all show just how deep the bonds between lovers and family members could be, even if some relationships started out as formal and unromantic arrangements. Love in the Middle Ages was a many-splendoured thing: chaste, passionate, messy, sublime, and everything in between.

Chapter Four

Nasty and Brutish

To conjure up a picture of the Middle Ages is inevitably to imagine something to do with violence, whether it's warfare, torture, or persecution. To 'get medieval' as a modern figure of speech *is* to be violent. While medieval Europe was certainly more violent than today in every sense (except for the vast destructive potential of our automatic and nuclear weapons, that is), our vision of the past is skewed both in terms of the amount of violence experienced in the course of everyday life and the rationale behind that violence.

Medieval justice and warfare could definitely be nasty, but it didn't tend to be brutish. Instead, what is simultaneously reassuring and horrifying is the sheer, rational nature of the decisions made around violence in both spheres. For better and for worse, a hard look at medieval attitudes towards violence makes the past seem much more familiar to our modern world than might be quite comfortable.

Wasn't the whole political structure of the Middle Ages based on 'might is right'?

Yes. Sort of. After the Roman Empire began to break up, its administrative and military structure collapsed, leaving a power vacuum. Invasions and migrations from the east redrew the boundaries of Europe at the same time as the people who had been oppressed under the Romans threw off their yokes. As a result, it was the people who had the potential to lead armies and protect communities who rose to power. That said, there were systems of justice in place, even early on, that made things a lot more fair than they might initially appear.

The feudal system grew out of the many conflicts that took place as Europe reformed itself. The new leaders – kings – were those men who had the backing of the people and could protect them from very real threats. People swore fealty to their kings, promising to be loyal, to serve, and to fight if they were called upon. In exchange, kings allowed the people to live on and work their land, and swore to protect them in the event of an attack. All the land within their borders belonged to medieval kings, which is why they were able to redistribute it at will; however, they had a fundamental and unbreakable responsibility to the people they led, which is why they were occasionally deposed. Kingship did not mean doing whatever you wanted – at least, not for long. The pact between a king and his people, though it was undeniably unequal, went both ways.

Aristocrats started out as those who could best support the king, financially, martially, and in terms of good counsel. Those positions became both entrenched and hereditary, just as other medieval classes and professions. Below the nobles were merchants, tradespeople, and artisans, and below them was the vast majority of the population: the peasant farmers, servants, and slaves.

> Another word used for peasants in the Middle Ages was *villein*, which, at the time, meant nothing more. In the days since, the word has been transformed into 'villain', inevitably the bad guy in any story, which tells you a little bit about the people who have been writing those stories in the centuries since.

There were slaves in medieval Europe?

Although they are not often discussed in terms of Europe, the idea being too distasteful to imagine, slaves were a part of medieval society for centuries.

One of the reasons Nordic peoples ('Vikings') raided so much and travelled so far was in search of slaves to capture and sell throughout Europe, down into the Middle East, and across to Russia. This is also one of the reasons why they were so feared by anyone who came into contact with them, including their own people. The modern word 'Slavs' derives from 'slaves', as these slaves were often other Nordic people. Archaeological artefacts show the extensive network of Nordic trade routes, with Middle Eastern coins found as far away as Finland. Some of the wares traded were people, which is just one of the reasons medieval Europe was a lot more ethnically diverse than has frequently been claimed.

> Although it's been hotly debated, one possible meaning of the word 'Viking' is raiding. The word *'Viking'* describes raiding in the summertime: it is an activity, not a group of people.

St Patrick was a slave himself, forcibly taken from his home in Britain as a teenager and taken to Ireland to work. His story is miraculous, but not in the way we traditionally tell it: in a stunning show of forgiveness, he deliberately returned to Ireland after he'd escaped captivity in order to convert his Irish captors. He didn't save them from snakes, he saved them from 'The Serpent': Satan.

Even though slavery dissipated over the course of the Middle Ages, there were plenty of unfree peasants or 'serfs' who were bound in service to the lord and had to obey him, abide by his justice, and ask his permission every time they wanted to leave his lands or get married.

When a serf got married, did the lord get to sleep with the bride?

No. The *jus primae noctis* ('right of first night') also called *prima nocta*, *le droit du seigneur*, or *le droit de cuissage* has been shown to be a myth. There is no evidence of it ever being practiced. Not even in fourteenth-century Scotland.

Lords did have a certain amount of power over their serfs' bodies in that they could order corporal punishments for legal infractions, but rape was not sanctioned by medieval law codes. Unfortunately it did still happen, just as it does today, and women of lower station were more vulnerable, their rapists punished more lightly, just as today.

Weren't punishments always pretty brutal?

Some of the punishments laid out in law codes were definitely gruesome, from blinding to severing tongues. That said, *most* punishments were financial or involved penance, so there weren't as many mutilated people (or headless ghosts) as a modern person might think.

Alfred the Great laid out a long and detailed list of punishments for crimes in Anglo-Saxon England, for example, most of them based around *wergeld*: the payment owed to the family of a person who was killed. People with higher positions required greater *wergeld* if their family members were murdered, but everyone had a price. These laws were put into place for the express purpose of avoiding violence and vendettas, and Alfred's precision indicates he was very invested in making sure that everyone was properly compensated. For example, losing a thumb required a payment of thirty shillings, while losing a little finger only nine (because it was less useful). Similarly, thirty shillings must be paid for cutting off someone's ear, and sixty if it means they lose the hearing. Alfred realised that people might hurt each other, and that punishment should be meted out; however, it was not necessary to take an eye for an eye and make the whole world blind.

Although there are other nasty laws on the books, and capital punishment was often recorded as being automatic even for what we might consider relatively small crimes like theft, this is not to say that people actually carried out those punishments in all – or even most – cases. While the law might have said that execution was fair, all over medieval Europe from Italy to England, people were resisting meting out corporal punishment and execution in favour of fines, imprisonment, or banishment.

It's important to remember that, unlike today's trials in which it's normal to not know the defendant or any of the other people in the courtroom, the people who were on all sides of a medieval case – defence, prosecution, jury, and sometimes judge – were usually neighbours. It's human nature to extend the benefit of the doubt towards people you know, and to treat them with lenience. In addition, there was also peer pressure to settle and make peace.

What about executions?

People took the commandment 'thou shalt not kill' very seriously, so they were not as trigger-happy when it came to criminals as modern media would lead us to believe. A quick look at the comments section on the news coverage of any crime today shows the deep divisions in modern society about how guilt should be determined, and what punishment a person deserves. It was the same in the Middle Ages: people disagreed over guilt, punishment, and how best to interpret the law, which meant that executions were far less common – and usually less gruesome – than we might imagine.

The purpose of execution has always been partly punishment, and partly removing a threat from the community. In order to do both, medieval people frequently sentenced criminals to banishment or exile. While this kept the townspeople's hands clean of blood, it had the unfortunate downside of filling the woods with outlaws that had nothing left to lose. (This is why Robin Hood had so many men in his merry band.) Outlaws were meant to be punished or killed if they were seen again; however, skilled or immoral outlaws could live for a long time in the woods, hunting or stealing what they needed. They could also move to another place where they were unknown, although they might not be welcomed there as strangers. Either way, the town or country that exiled them didn't have to deal with them anymore or shed their blood. Win/win.

When people were executed, it was traitors who received the worst deaths, such as hanging, drawing and quartering, with the quartered parts of the body being sent across the country to serve as a warning, and the head placed on a spike. This was the famous method of execution meted out to William Wallace in 1305 CE, and it was meant to be a horrific example to subdue people in those rebellious parts of Great Britain who were not otherwise afraid to fight and die to keep their lands, namely Scotland and Wales. It has gone down in history as terrible, exactly as it was meant to.

Heretics were increasingly burned, but while it was definitely a painful way to die, pain was not necessarily the goal. The goal was purification – of the person and of the community – through fire, just as Christians believed God purified souls. Considerate townspeople, relatives, and executioners would often speed the deaths of those condemned to burning by placing more fuel or smoky materials on the pyre to allow the person to die of smoke inhalation before they were engulfed. In either case, the person died and the body was destroyed in a particularly symbolic punishment.

All this being said, most executions were simple hangings, a method still in use today in some parts of the world. Medieval hangings were worse than more recent hangings, however, in that they had not begun to use the later trap-door gallows. Instead of a quick drop that snapped the person's neck (provided the executioner correctly tied the noose), medieval hangings involved strangulation, a much slower process.

Executions were, indeed, public events, but it's important to understand that they were more than just a place for a mob to witness something disturbing for the sake of sadistic pleasure. Public execution was a complex mix of curiosity, catharsis, and religious experience in which a person witnessed first-hand the type of human suffering so central to medieval Christianity (not only the passion of Jesus, but the suffering of martyrs). It was a moment when someone's soul crossed over into the afterlife, a transition which people spent a lot of time thinking about in terms of their own lives. It was also a moment in which the full power of the law was made visible in its terrible justice, bringing relief and dread. Tempting as it might be, to imagine a crowd of uniformly callous or cruel people eagerly awaiting the first sign of pain is to oversimplify medieval people's minds and hearts.

In order to avoid making the wrong decision when someone's life was at stake, people in the Early Middle Ages left the decision up to God by using trial by combat, and trial by ordeal. It's likely that even though these were meant to be just intense tests, those in the middle of these trials must have felt they were almost worse than the punishment, itself.

How did trial by combat and trial by ordeal work?

Trial by combat was relatively straightforward: whoever won the fight (accuser or accused) had proved that God was on their side, and that they had spoken the truth. In certain cases, a champion was required to fight the battle on behalf of one of the parties, which led to some people making a dangerous living as professional champions. Some criminals even took on the work in the medieval version of a 'plea deal'. Once professional champions stepped in and muddied the waters, it was more difficult than ever to see God's hand at work in the outcome. Trial by combat gradually died out, although it was occasionally still in practice up until the late fourteenth century.

In a trial by ordeal, the accused was usually made to perform some injurious deed, with the healing or festering of the resulting wound indicating God's verdict. For example, the accused may have had to carry a hot vessel between his or her arms from one point to another, or to grab a stone from the bottom of a pot of boiling holy water. The resulting burn was then wrapped in a cloth and sealed with a judge's signet ring. If, a few days later, the wound was seen to be healing cleanly, the person was innocent. If it became infected, the person was guilty. Another ordeal was to have a priest bless a body of water – usually a pit made expressly for this purpose – and to throw the accused into it, just as in Early Modern witch trials. If the holy water rejected the accused, they were guilty. Those who sank were innocent, although they sometimes drowned anyway.

As a side benefit, people involved in these trials were punished for ever letting themselves be implicated in a crime no matter what the outcome, but the tricky thing about trial by combat and trial by ordeal was that it was difficult to interpret God's justice. People were not stupid: they knew you could weigh the odds in your favour exponentially with simple tricks. Because it was decided that testing God was not a great idea (especially in light of criminals being able to 'cheat' the system), at the Fourth Lateran Council, Innocent III forbade priests to take part in ordeals or to bless the instruments of them. Fortunately, the justice system was already leaving them by the wayside.

How did the justice system work after that?

In its simplest form, the medieval legal system all over Europe was divided into two halves: the secular court and the ecclesiastical court.

60   Life in Medieval Europe: Fact and Fiction

The ecclesiastical court was ruled by the church, and it had jurisdiction over all of its clergy. The secular court worked within the king's law and had jurisdiction over everyone else. Even with these distinctions, though, things were a bit messy: crimes against the church – such as adultery, blasphemy, and heresy – were tried by the ecclesiastical court, while crimes against society – theft, murder, and rape, for example – were tried by the secular court. The ecclesiastical court doled out mostly penance and humiliations for crimes and was not permitted to shed the blood of the convicted. The secular court fined people, sentenced them to corporal punishment or imprisonment, or executed them. If the ecclesiastical court required someone be executed, such as Joan of Arc, it would pass her over to the secular court under the charge of treason (heresy being considered to be just as bad for society as outright betraying the country), washing its hands of the deed but getting it done, anyway.

An additional wrinkle which made things tense was that anyone who was trained by the church to be one of its clergy, even in the lower orders, automatically fell under ecclesiastical law. This meant that while an ordinary person who committed murder could be hanged for it, a clerk who committed murder was simply given penance.

> To prove that you had the 'benefit of clergy' you were usually required to recite the *Paternoster* (Lord's Prayer) in Latin. Unsurprisingly, clever criminals who had never seen the inside of a church quickly learned their *Paternosters* in order to escape the harsher punishments of royal justice.

This system of different punishments for the same crime, and the abuse of the benefit of clergy, really began to grind the gears of England's Henry II in the twelfth century. He appointed his friend, Thomas Becket, to the position of Archbishop of Canterbury because he believed that Becket would help him to reform the system – to the benefit of the king's justice, of course. Once he (reluctantly) took up the position, however, Becket stubbornly refused to cooperate in bringing the clergy under secular law. This was the crux of the troubles between the two powerful men that eventually led to Becket's martyrdom. Henry's dreams of one law for all died along with Becket, and the rest of Europe took note of the fallout. Still, Henry did succeed in tightening up other aspects of English law to more closely resemble the system used today.

In medieval trials, people who testified were asked to swear on the gospels that their testimony was true (Jewish witnesses swore on the Torah). Witnesses were questioned and both questions and answers were recorded by a court clerk. Once all testimony had been heard and forensic evidence examined, the judge or jury made their decision. Overall, people trusted in this centralised justice system, which was one of the reasons being tried by 'the legal judgement of [a person's] peers' was (unwillingly) enshrined in Magna Carta by Henry's son John.

They used forensic evidence?

Yes. It would be a mistake to assume that medieval people didn't notice things like suspicious injuries, torn clothing, paint smears, or the marks of a weapon. After all, they regularly had to notice and interpret tiny details in their natural environments in order to feed themselves. As today, forensic evidence was sometimes the key to ascertaining a person's guilt or innocence.

When someone was the victim of a crime, or discovered that one had been committed, he or she immediately raised the 'hue and cry', which meant that everyone in the community was legally required to stop what they were doing and come to that person's aid. Because there was no centralised police force, the idea was that the quick response meant the crowd could run down criminals and apprehend them. Many times, however, a crime was discovered long enough after the fact that the crime scene had to be examined for clues, just like today.

Although the church did not permit autopsies, when a suspicious death occurred, doctors or coroners examined the body for clues whenever possible. In one trial record from southern France, a young wife, Margarida de Portu, was accused by her brother-in-law of murdering her husband Johan through poison and sorcery. A local doctor examined the corpse and testified that Johan had not been poisoned, as there was no evidence of poison apparent on the body. Instead, he concluded, Johan had died of a heart attack. Margarida was cleared – mostly, that is. The good doctor testified that Margarida had caused her husband's heart attack by refusing to sleep with him: all of Johan's pent-up sexual frustration proved to be fatal. Fortunately for Margarida, refusing to sleep with your spouse – although grounds for an annulment – was not a crime. She was free to go. Margarida's story not only demonstrates that forensic examinations were performed, but that a person could be charged with murder, and even sorcery, and be cleared by the justice system.

If people didn't confess to their crimes, were they tortured?

It depended on where that person lived. In most of Europe, including Germany, Italy, Spain, Flanders, and France, torture was an accepted part of the legal system in both secular and ecclesiastical law. In England, torture was illegal under secular law. It's not a surprise, then, that Templars on the Continent – especially in France, where inquisitors were under express instructions from Philip the Fair to use torture – confessed to all manner of crimes, while English Templars did not.

While people may have accepted torture as a means to getting to the truth, they did not accept it being used arbitrarily. Even in France, where torture was legal, it was forbidden to torture someone if they were accused of a crime by just one witness; torture was not meant to be used for vengeance, but for justice. Many people also recognised that a person under torture will say just about anything, which meant that their testimony was unreliable. This was the crux of Edward II's argument against allowing the Templars under his jurisdiction to be tortured; he did not believe that truth could be found that way (although he eventually bowed under the pressure and allowed it).

Believe it or not, most 'medieval' torture devices are actually clever Victorian fakes meant to convince people of the barbarism of the Middle Ages. The iron maiden, the pear of anguish, and the infamous chastity belt are not medieval and were never used. Even the scold's bridle is Early Modern. When medieval people wanted to torture someone, they didn't need elaborate means to do it. The Templars were tortured using simple techniques: being slowly starved, hung by their arms by a *strappado*, or burned on the soles of their feet. Even more simply, they were tortured by the threat of having to stay indefinitely imprisoned in a dungeon, and by the psychological wear and tear of constant interrogation. Of course they confessed.

It's tempting to distance ourselves from the torture of the Middle Ages, but we know from our most recent wars that people today are still tortured in secret in the hope of extracting confessions when it comes to serious threats to national security, as medieval people believed both treason and heresy to be. While the methods are different, the same rationale has been applied.

Weren't medieval people always fighting?

Although skirmishes and battles happened fairly regularly throughout the Middle Ages, they certainly were not everyday occurrences. During much of the Middle Ages, most kingdoms didn't even have standing armies of professional soldiers. There were a couple of reasons for this: first, the medieval political system built military support into its oral contract, so it was always possible for a king to call up troops should he have need, and second, to have a standing army is to feed, clothe, and house them, as well as to keep them out of trouble in times of peace. When warfare became more frequent – for example, during the Hundred Years War – kings needed to hire mercenaries more often to get the skill sets they needed. Unfortunately, these large groups of mercenaries brought with them all the troubles of a standing army without the loyalty. After this point (the very end of the Middle Ages) it seemed wise to have regular, trained soldiers.

Although people weren't always fighting, medieval culture in general was undeniably martial. War was not the only thing a nobleman was trained to know about – he was required to run his estates, be a fair and wise judge to his people and counsellor to his king, as well as to increase his wealth – but military capability was an essential part of his identity, and a necessary component of his vassalage. Even the men in the lower estates were expected to know their way around weapons and to supply them whenever necessary. For peasants, easily accessible weapons could be clubs, daggers, bows, and everyday tools, such as axes and hammers. Armour was a quilted or boiled leather jacket, a helmet, and possibly a shield. Although people were expected to own their own military equipment, records suggest that kings would outfit their armies when they called them up to make up for any missing gear. The lower classes didn't always have the opportunity to be well-trained, depending on how long they had been together on campaign, and how many times they'd been called up, but they were often assigned to be the front lines, using pikes, bows, daggers, and (later) guns.

Was the longbow really that deadly?

The English longbow was 6 ft long, usually made of yew, and deadly at 200 yards. It was easy to make and relatively easy to learn, although it took years to build up the strength to pull one. Bows that were discovered on the shipwrecked Tudor vessel the *Mary Rose* have been recreated in size and weight, and it's estimated that some of them had draw weights (that is, the amount of pull required to draw the string back fully) of over 150 lbs. Arrows shot from English longbows could both split chainmail and puncture plate mail. They were every bit as deadly as you might imagine.

In the midst of the Hundred Years War, Edward III of England outlawed the playing of all sports on people's days off in favour of archery, either with longbows or crossbows. Because crossbows were more expensive and harder to obtain, most of the population used longbows. Edward's idea was to give himself a massive pool of archers to choose from when gathering armies for new attacks in France. Although this can't have been a popular law, Edward's unpopularity paid off, especially for the outnumbered, starving, and sick troops of Henry V more than half a century later, whose skill with the longbow allowed them to survive the killing fields of Agincourt.

> Archery targets were called butts, which is why someone who is the target of a joke is still called the 'butt' of the joke.

What about crossbows?

Crossbows were so deadly that Innocent III banned their use against other Christians (not that anyone paid attention). The bow arm (lath) could be made of wood or steel, or a combination of wood and bone, while the stock was wood with a trigger underneath. In order to pull back the bowstring, a foot was placed in the stirrup at the front, and sometimes a crank, lever, or winch was used. Once the bowstring was set at full draw, a bolt (quarrel) was loaded.

Crossbows were more powerful than longbows; however, the extremely heavy draw weight made them much slower to reload. Still, their power was worth the trade in some situations, such as sieges, during which crossbowmen might be more likely to have reliable cover while they reloaded. While the English had the most fearsome reputation with the longbow, it was the Italian (Genoese) mercenaries who were known to be deadliest with the crossbow.

What about knights?

Knights were a different class altogether, and required a lifetime of training, usually a noble pedigree, and a massive amount of equipment. While knighthoods could be – and were – granted on the field, it was unkind for a king to knight a commoner unless he was willing to help him afford the kit he needed.

> Knights were called *chevaliers* in French, from the word for horse (*cheval*). This is also where we get the word for knightly behaviour: chivalry.

The most obvious mark of a knight was his horse. A knight's warhorse was called a destrier and was trained not only to be fearless in the midst of the sounds, sights, and smells of the battlefield, but also to be a partner to his rider. Destriers were trained to stomp, kick, bite, and charge directly into combat. This isn't to say that the horses were never afraid; occasionally they caused all kinds of havoc through the sheer terror of being injured and trapped in the midst of a battle. Rather, the best destriers were strong, agile, well-trained, and courageous. They were extremely valuable and expensive, which is why it was so painful for a knight to lose one at a tournament.

The skills required to both win a battle and hold onto your horse at tournament were honed by daily practice. Knights spent hours tilting at quintains with lances in imitation of the cavalry charges they'd be required to perform on the battlefield. Quintains were wooden t-shaped posts that were capable of swivelling on a central axis. A target was attached to the end of one of the quintain's arms, with a weight (like a sandbag) attached to the other. If a knight's lance hit the quintain's target at the right angle and speed, it would swing around harmlessly. If he missed or rode too slowly, the sandbag swung around and hit him, sometimes knocking him from his horse.

Of course, once a knight was off his horse (whether by accident or by design), he had to know how to fight on foot using swords, poleaxes, and daggers. Late-medieval two-handed swords could be over 3 ft long, although it was sometimes more practical to use shorter 'bastard swords', so called because they could be used either one-handed or two-handed. Even if a knight's sword failed to pierce his opponent's armour, the weight of his blow could still cause internal damage. Knights were most vulnerable at the gaps in their armour: neck, face, and groin. Neck and face wounds were, of course, often fatal, and a stab or slash to the groin could cut the femoral artery, meaning the enemy would bleed out quickly and die on the field.

Full armour for a late medieval knight involved quite a lot of equipment. On top of his tunic and hose, he'd wear a quilted aketon to absorb some of the impact from blows and to keep his armour from chafing. Then he'd put on a mail shirt (hauberk), a mail hood (coif), and mail leggings. After this, metal plates would be attached to his body by leather straps, covering him from shoulder to toes. Finally, he'd put on gloves and his helmet, as well as possibly a surcoat or tabard: a loose-fitting tunic featuring his heraldic colours and symbols which was meant to identify the person who was concealed under all that metal.

> Medieval people called chainmail 'mail' and plate mail 'plate'. While we tend to call the former 'chainmail' today, medieval people would find that redundant.

Could they even move under all that armour?

The modern idea that it was impossible to move in armour is surprising, since common sense dictates that a knight who was immobile as soon as he fell off his horse was immediately going to be killed. Believe it or not, knights were capable of a huge range of movement, even fully armed. The biographer of Jean II le Meingre – better known as Boucicaut – explains what Boucicaut's training in full armour entailed:

> He would train himself to leap fully armed onto his horse's back, or on other occasions he would go for long runs on foot, to increase his strength and resistance, or he would train for hours with a battle-axe or a hammer to harden himself to armour and to exercise his arms and hands, so that he could easily raise his arms when fully armed … he could do a full somersault fully armed but for his [helmet], and he could dance equipped in a coat of mail.

Other things Boucicaut could do were to climb between two walls 'the height of a tower', as well as to climb the underside of a 'ladder leaning against a wall', using just his hands. Although Boucicaut's biographer is trying to make him sound impressive – mostly by the sheer amount of work and time he put in – these were all things an armed knight was capable of, as modern reconstructive archaeology has shown.

It is true that heavily armed knights were more vulnerable in one sense: they were very much at risk of drowning. Many knights died while fighting at river crossings or on marshy ground, as they were unable to surface or were trampled facedown into the muck.

Did knights get to use their skills often?

Although much knightly training was to prepare them for mounted cavalry charges, the majority of medieval warfare was conducted in the form of sieges, so some knights probably used their horsemanship more often on the tournament field than the battlefield. Pitched battles in which one army charges headlong at another are so unpredictable that an army which is both outnumbered and underequipped can still manage to win despite all odds, as history has shown time and time again. Castles, with their strong walls and many defences, made it much easier to fend off an attack, and as such they were the place where most conflicts came to a head.

The first castles were built in a 'motte and bailey' style. A motte was a raised hill, either natural or man-made, on which a tower would be built. At the bottom of the hill was an area called the bailey in which all of the necessary buildings needed to support the tower – such as smithies, stables, and barracks – were fenced in by a palisade. As time went on, defences grew in ever increasing concentric circles, leading to the establishment of 'inner baileys' and 'outer baileys'. Even at their most elaborate, castles still tended to have a layout in which defenders could fall back from outer defences as they were taken, until eventually defenders could seek refuge behind the walls of the strong inner tower or 'keep'. Although the keep was often the home of the lord who owned the castle, keep walls were built several metres thick as a testament to their other role as the last line of defence.

> Prisoners would be taken to a castle's keep and kept under guard. The French word for keep – *donjon* – is what gives us the English word 'dungeon'.

How did a siege work?

Once a castle's occupants knew they were about to be besieged, they closed themselves in, raising drawbridges, and lowering massive gates called portcullises. Then they gathered what weapons they could, organised supplies, and waited. Archers and lookouts were posted to the walls where they could take shelter behind the crenellations – those regular, rectangular parts at the top of a castle's walls that look like teeth and give castles their traditional distinctive silhouette.

Besiegers ranged themselves in front of the walls wherever it seemed the castle was weakest, carefully keeping their camp out of bowshot. If at all possible, it was best to completely surround the castle, so that there was no chance for the defenders to get supplies or to escape through a back door, but a scarcity of manpower and resources often meant a focused attack.

One of the most effective ways to breach a castle's defences was 'undermining': digging under a wall or a tower and then collapsing the tunnel, bringing the wall down with it. Needless to say, this was also an extremely dangerous undertaking, in that the miners were in continual danger from the defenders' arrows while they did their work, and they were at risk of the tunnel collapsing while they were still in it. Still, whenever the soil permitted, undermining was a common tactic. Sometimes, defenders even built countermines in order to head off the attackers – bloody battles were fought where the two tunnels met.

A famous example of undermining was chronicled in England during the civil war that followed King John's rejection of the Magna Carta. In his siege of Rochester Castle, John's miners dug a tunnel under the south tower, keeping it propped up by wooden beams, before smearing the beams with pig fat and setting them ablaze. The tower collapsed, although the rebels still managed to hold out for a couple of months. John's son, Henry III, rebuilt Rochester Castle's south tower years later, this time in a newer, stronger style: instead of the four original square Norman towers, Rochester Castle still features one round tower to this day. Round towers were built to better withstand increasingly powerful siege engines, including a new and terrifying weapon: the counterweight trebuchet.

What is a trebuchet?

Trebuchets are an adaptation of a sling, albeit on a massive scale. The throwing arm has a box loaded with a huge amount of weight in the form of sandbags or stone attached at one end, and a sling attached to the other. The weighted end is winched into the air while the sling is loaded with a heavy projectile, usually a huge stone. When the weight is released, the box swings down, flinging the sling upwards where one end slips off and the projectile is thrown towards the target.

The trebuchet was a truly fearsome weapon. Calibrating one can be tricky – too much weight or too little, too much friction on the sling or too little and the trebuchet can shoot its projectile straight up, or even backwards. That said, once it is calibrated, a trebuchet is extremely accurate and reliable, easily bringing down a tower or wall over a relatively short amount of time (depending on its size) without the besiegers needing to get close. Some chronicle accounts mention only a few stones being thrown from a trebuchet before defenders surrendered. The biggest ever recorded was called 'Warwolf' and it was built by Edward I's army to besiege Stirling Castle. The Scots took one look at it and surrendered before a shot was fired, but Edward made them stay inside long enough for him to test it out.

Trebuchets had the additional benefit of being able to throw over the walls, not just into them. This was useful, as they could be loaded up with flaming projectiles which set the wooden buildings of a castle bailey ablaze as they landed. Even worse, trebuchets could be used for psychological and biological warfare. There are chronicled cases of heads and bodies being thrown over walls, including one instance in which the Mongols threw the corpses of those who had been infected with the Black Death into the city of Caffa in order to infect the people inside.

What else did besiegers do to get in?

In tandem with undermining and using siege engines, attackers would be performing direct assaults. Joan of Arc in particular favoured this tactic, as it seemed to take her enemies by surprise: instead of waiting for the cannons to do their work, she put herself in harm's way by throwing herself at the walls. This unorthodox technique may have been the key to her early successes, such as at Orléans, but it left her injured more than once.

Attackers, under the covering fire of their archers, brought ladders – such as that described by Boucicaut's biographer – to get themselves up the walls. They could also use grappling hooks and ropes. Each of these methods required extreme courage, as attackers were very vulnerable as they climbed, both from attacks on themselves, and on their ladders and ropes. Once they made it to the top of the walls, they were still vulnerable to falling off them while clearing a path for those scaling the ladders behind them.

A safer, if more complicated, alternative was to build siege towers or 'belfries': wooden towers on wheels that could be rolled up to a castle's walls. These towers were usually covered in urine-soaked hides to prevent them from catching fire. Once the belfries were rolled into place, attackers could climb up the interior ladders without worrying about being hacked apart or pushed off the walls.

If attackers were able to breach the gates, either by fire or with the use of a battering ram, there were more dangers within. Usually, castle gates had entryways with two portcullises, meaning that those who breached the outer gate still had to get past the inner one. Meanwhile, 'murder holes' in the ceiling above this entryway allowed defenders to drop stones, boiling water, and hot sand onto the attackers below without being especially vulnerable to counterattack. Pouring boiling oil was a waste of precious fuel (and risking setting fire to one's own walls that way was a bad idea) but boiling water did just as well at scalding attackers, and hot sand got between all the tiny cracks in an enemy's armour to burn and itch terribly. Even if the attackers got past this wall, chances were there was another curtain wall, or the great stone walls of the keep to contend with.

One of the most successful ways to win a siege, however, was not necessarily to fight it. Medieval warriors knew that as long as they cut off the supplies to a castle, eventually those within would starve to death – or at least turn on each other and surrender to prevent dying of starvation. Unfortunately, the waiting game was a race against the clock for both the defenders and the attackers, as the besieging forces had to keep their armies fed for just as long. Also, winter weather and disease were constant concerns, which meant that many a siege was lifted because the weather was too bad or the besiegers too sick to continue.

Did anyone fight pitched battles?

Yes. Some of the most famous battles of the Middle Ages (Crécy, Hastings, Aljubarrota) were pitched battles, which is probably why we tend to think these were the most common. However, pitched battles are celebrated in large part because the victors were so very relieved that they turned out well.

Pitched battles turned not just on the size and equipment of the armies, but on the weather, food supply, and health of the armies – just as in siege warfare – as well as the terrain. The ideal battlefield was one in which your army had the higher, drier ground, with natural defences at your sides and the sun at your back. But even with any or all of these advantages on your side, like at Hastings, the outcome was still not a forgone conclusion.

Battles usually began with ranged weapons as one army approached the other. The defenders still standing after the rain of arrows would brace themselves against attack, creating a wall of pikes and shields to stab infantry and repel cavalry. Cavalry could swing around and ride down the opposing army from the sides, although it was important that both sides kept attackers from getting behind their lines. If the wall of infantry was strong, it could push back the attackers; if it fell apart, everyone was in it for themselves.

While the sophisticated battle strategies of intelligent leaders were all well and good (and many of them were ingenious) just as often it happened that all hell broke loose and everyone did the best they could to stay alive. Contrary to popular belief, people did not just throw down their weapons the second someone captured a king: battles were fought to the bitter, bloody end, as the recently discovered body of Richard III bears witness. Medieval people were not playing with sticks and stones, and they were not always noble; they were fighting to the death, and they did whatever they needed to do in order to make it out alive.

Chivalric tradition required that nobles be captured and ransomed, ransoms being a handy way to raise money for more war while ensuring your enemy was underfunded. Even people of lesser stations were sometimes ransomed, although they were more often killed because their ransoms would have been too small to matter. Despite his reputation as a well-beloved king, Henry V shocked Europe when he ordered all his French captives killed at Agincourt regardless of their station or potential ransoms. Whether he felt it was the only way to escape, or whether it was vengeance, some have called this moment the death of chivalry.

Were guns invented in the Middle Ages?

More than the purported death of chivalry above, what changed warfare forever was the appearance of firearms in Europe. Although Asian peoples had known about gunpowder for centuries, Europeans only started using cannons in the early fourteenth century. Like so many other technological advances, it's hard to know when and where the first cannons were invented, but once they came into being, use of them spread like wildfire.

Early cannons made it possible to break down the walls of enemy fortresses just as fast or faster than trebuchets, and they were much smaller, easier to manoeuvre and aim, and (relatively) lighter. While cannons didn't require the dangerous step of raising an enormously heavy weight into the air, they were still likely to misfire and kill the operators. Because they were made of iron and bronze, early cannons are rare archaeological finds; old cannons were simply melted down for recasting.

Muskets were also beginning to be used near the end of the Middle Ages, and (when they worked) they were deadly, piercing the plate armour that had proved so effective against swords. Eventually, it seemed redundant to even wear plate if most of the fighting was done at a distance. Swords were still in use – the famous French musketeers of the Early Modern period carried swords in addition to their muskets – but they became smaller: rapiers became more popular than longswords, and a new style of swordplay was born. There was no longer a need for a huge sword when your opponent wasn't wearing plate armour. The formidable medieval archer was also replaced over time by the rifleman, as once you had a big enough arsenal, it was easy to teach anyone to point and shoot.

Medieval warfare was undeniably ugly, but then again, war is horrific by its very definition. This chapter has looked at some of the nastiest aspects of life in medieval Europe, and while perhaps it's fair to judge any society by its worst moments, it seems unfair to judge the Middle Ages by its violence unless we're willing to apply the same standards to recent history (an uncomfortable idea).

What's important to remember when reflecting on medieval justice (if not warfare) is that the focus *was* on justice, not violence for its own sake or for the sake of entertainment. People actively tried to avoid corporal punishments and execution if matters could be settled by fines or banishment, and being accused didn't necessarily mean being convicted. Although it would make for much less dramatic movies and books to see this information make its way into popular culture, medieval attitudes towards violence were not as brutish – or unfamiliar – as they might initially seem.

Chapter Five

The Age of Faith

The Middle Ages is often called 'The Age of Faith' because of a modern belief that the hearts and minds of the medieval world were ruled by faith alone, without question or doubt, and with little tolerance for error. The curious nature of humans, however, makes it difficult for any of us to do just about anything without questions, doubts, or errors, let alone lead our whole lives that way.

While it's true that the Catholic church was more powerful than it has been either before or since, there was wide variation in medieval beliefs, as well as in people's tolerance for religious differences (big and small). Theologians spent much of their time debating and ironing out the exact rules for good Christians to follow, and although Christianity was the dominant religion, it was by no means the only one practiced in medieval Europe. Jewish communities existed in many medieval towns, and for centuries Spain and Portugal were Muslim. Much to the disgust of purists from all three religions, cross-pollination of ideas frequently occurred through universities, in the marketplace, and on crusade. No matter how many clarifications and orders were issued by the papacy, faith in the Middle Ages was a complex, messy tangle of tolerance and intolerance, belief and doubt.

Was medieval Europe ruled by the church?

Yes, and no. While most of the big decisions in Europe were made by kings and queens, there was no separation of kingship and religion in the Middle Ages. Medieval kings and queens ruled by 'divine right'; that is, they were believed to have been appointed to their station by God, who authorised their actions. In coronation ceremonies, it was the archbishop who placed the crown on the king's head after anointing him with oils. From that moment on, the king's body was holy.

> The 'royal we' – when monarchs refer to themselves as 'we' instead of 'I' – is a throwback to the days in which it was believed that an anointed king was more than just a man: he was part divine.

Despite kings and queens being touched by the divine, until the Reformation the pope was considered the ultimate authority on Earth, meaning that even royalty was supposed to bend to his will and obey his edicts. This is not to say that kings were above putting huge amounts of pressure on popes to get them to see things their way, however. Philip the Fair of France leaned heavily on Pope Clement V to get him to disband the Templars, even going so far as to place his army within striking distance of Clement's palace as he deliberated.

Popes influenced all aspects of medieval kingship and government, from blessing or disapproving of marriages by waiving or upholding issues of consanguinity, to placing whole kingdoms under interdict, to calling for crusades, to brokering peace between nations. During the Hundred Years' War, when there were two popes – one in Rome and one in Avignon – the nations of Europe divided themselves along both political and spiritual lines. Even at the level of king versus archbishop, spiritual power was mighty; when Henry II of England (accidentally or purposefully) sanctioned the murder of the Archbishop of Canterbury, Thomas Becket, he was made to humble himself as penance by walking barefoot to Becket's tomb, and allowing himself to be struck on the back by over eighty members of the clergy.

When Henry VIII split with Rome and took the pope's authority for himself centuries later, he not only changed the faith of his nation, he set a precedent that was to change the power structure of Europe.

How did people practice their faith?

Christianity permeated every part of daily life. Europe was divided geographically into parishes, each one in the care of a bishop who saw to his flock's spiritual needs. This was easier said than done in rural areas. They were often served by itinerant priests who would walk a circuit of the area preaching sermons and performing the sacraments. For practical reasons, people weren't required to attend weekly mass in order to be saved. The minimum requirement was confession and communion once per year at Easter.

Prayer and ritual were woven into the fabric of the everyday, from saying grace before meals, to wearing rosary beads, to eating fish on Fridays. One of the most frequent points of contact with Christianity was in the way people told time. Throughout medieval Europe, church bells rang out at regular intervals to announce the canonical hours: the correct times to pray or sing certain parts of the liturgy. The canonical hours were not actually at one-hour intervals, but further apart, starting with Matins in the very early (pre-dawn) morning, then Lauds, Prime, Tierce, Sext, Nones, Vespers, and Compline after dark. Monks and nuns were expected to sing their prayers at every ringing of the bells, even through the night, which is why some abbeys had built-in 'night stairs' from the dormitories to the sanctuary, so the monks and nuns could roll out of bed and down to worship. Ordinary people were not required to lose sleep in favour of prayer unless they had some serious repenting to do.

In addition to the hours being calculated by religious practice, the days were, too. Sunday was, of course, the day of rest, and the day on which weekly masses were held, but there were many other holy days to observe. Western communities still celebrate the major ones, such as Christmas and Easter, but there were several other important holy days, such as Michaelmas, Candlemas, Corpus Christi, Pentecost, and saints' days. Many of these important days called for celebration and feasting, and no work was permitted on holy days, which is why the word 'holiday' is still associated with taking the day off.

Alfred the Great set out the following holiday schedule for his people:

> Let these days be given to all freemen, but not to slaves or the unfree: twelve days at Christmas, and the day on which Christ overcame the devil, and the commemoration day of St. Gregory, and the seven days before Easter and seven

78   Life in Medieval Europe: Fact and Fiction

days after, and one day at the feast of St. Peter and St. Paul, and during the harvest the whole week before the feast of St. Mary, and one day at the celebration of All Saints.

This number of regular holidays rivals many modern vacation-day allotments, meaning these Anglo-Saxon freemen were often free men, indeed.

> In medieval calendars, the major holy feasts and festivals were written down in red ink: they were red-letter days.

Despite popular belief, science, technology, and faith were not mutually exclusive. Clocks, hourglasses, and candles made it easy for priests to tell what time it was in order to pray. The complicated astrolabe, which made navigation possible and depended heavily on Islamic geometric calculations, was not seen as a diabolical instrument. While autopsies were not permitted, forensic analysis of human remains was used to solve crimes. Wind- and watermills made it possible for monasteries to grind grain for the wider community, and even the four Evangelists are frequently depicted in books of hours wearing a new-fangled piece of technology: eyeglasses. Roger Bacon, a monk, was one of the most forward-thinking scientists in Europe, and many of the most advanced thinkers in all of the medieval world were Muslim.

Where science and faith clashed most grievously was in the debate over the arrangement of the universe. Theologians believed that Jerusalem was the centre of everything; that is, the universe rotated around it. (Medieval maps of the world are consistently drawn with Jerusalem in the middle.) This made sense from a theological perspective, though not a scientific one. It wasn't until well after the medieval period, however, that Galileo was famously persecuted by the church.

Who took care of people's spiritual needs?

Clergy in medieval Europe were divided into two groups: secular clergy, who went among the people, and regular clergy, who were cloistered and lived according to a rule (*regula*). Secular clergy were involved in the day-to-day lives of the people, from working as priests and clerks, to holding office as bishops and archbishops. Regular clergy were meant to be tucked away in their cloisters to live a life of seclusion and contemplation, although in reality they were much more a part of the community than this neat division indicates.

Priests were usually attached to one church or private chapel to perform masses and to minister to the community, and they were assisted in their duties by clerics of lower orders (such as deacons and archdeacons). Only those ordained as priests could administer the sacraments, themselves. Clerics who had been educated but not ordained could serve in other capacities, and often found work in either political or religious administration because of their ability to read and write.

What was it like to be a monk or a nun?

The vast majority of monastic orders required their members to take vows of poverty, chastity, and obedience, although the different orders disagreed with each other on how best to serve God, mainly attempting to outdo each other in austerity. Despite the differences in their philosophies, most religious houses were run according to *The Rule of St Benedict*, which outlined everything from food to clothing to how often to bathe, as we've seen elsewhere in this book.

Although they were meant to be cloistered and separate from the community as much as possible, some monks were ordained, which meant that they could be called upon to perform masses and last rites when a priest was not available. It also meant that these monks were not always as removed from the world as they might wish, and that mendicant friars who wandered to preach, like Franciscans, had something to trade for food and shelter.

The ideal self-sustaining monastery outlined in the ninth-century Plan of St Gall was meant to hold 300 people – both monks and lay brothers (those who did not take vows) – on a small plot of land. With the assistance of lay brothers, monks were expected to work in between prayers to keep the monastery going. Beyond the standard requirements, such as places for the brothers to eat, sleep, and pray, the Plan of St Gall includes:

> the infirmary, houses for physicians, and a medicinal herb garden ... [a] cemetery and orchard, monks' vegetable garden, and chicken and goose houses ... mill, mortar, drying kiln, workshops, and no fewer than three bake and brew houses.

The plan also made space for a library and a well-lit *scriptorium* for the monks, as well as space for the laymen, namely 'fowl-keepers, shoemakers, goldsmiths, coopers, grooms, millers, and shepherds'. While not every monastery would have had all of these amenities and workshops, looking at the ideal gives us a sense of what was important enough to be included to meet the day-to-day needs of a monastic community.

Weren't monasteries also schools?

Yes. Beyond being central hubs of faith and community, monasteries and cathedrals were centres of learning. It was clergy who educated the next generation for careers in administration or lives as priests, adding a further layer of spiritual commitment to the governing process. Many times, a chancellor was also a bishop or archbishop, as those were some of the most learned men of the time; they had had the most formal education, and their education was via the church.

St Benedict considered 'divine reading' to be a primary duty of the regular clergy. In fact, he decreed, 'On Sundays, everyone should be free for reading, except those assigned to various duties'. He also suggests certain monks should patrol the reading areas to make sure no one is distracting the other monks from their books. A repeat distractor should be punished 'in such a way that the others are afraid', a rule that may not sound all that unreasonable to some avid readers today.

Convents were places in which women's learning was encouraged too, so that they could better understand holy texts. For many women who did not wish for a life of marriage and children, convents were a sanctuary in which they could spend their days learning and discussing theology. Great thinkers and writers such as Hildegard von Bingen were able to thrive in such an environment. Often, widows chose to retire to convents rather than remarry, especially if there was a risk that they might not be able to choose their next husbands, themselves. For these women, many of whom would have been literate, having lifelong access to a convent's library must've seemed a heavenly option, indeed.

The emphasis on reading in monasteries and convents made them hives of learning and disseminating information beyond just the classroom, as it was monastic communities who did the lion's share of the copying of books in early medieval Europe, especially religious texts. Monasteries frequently had *scriptoria*: rooms in which monks would copy and illuminate books to be kept in their libraries, given, or sold. Sometimes, the monks who copied these books were literate enough to also absorb the information in them; other times, illiterate monks simply copied the letter forms, leading to the medieval version of typos.

Some learned monks took it upon themselves to write history, as well, chronicling the lives and happenings of their own communities, as well as the world outside. Historians today are immensely grateful for these contemporary accounts, although they do have to be taken with a grain of salt. That is, praise or condemnation of the people – especially women – in the accounts needs to be viewed through the lens of the values of both the time and the writer's perspective as a monk.

Weren't there a lot of stories about saints in the Middle Ages?

Saints were the superheroes of the Middle Ages, their morals pure, and their powers varied and immense. Often tortured by horribly cruel pagans, the saints endured unspeakable pain and humiliation with serenity and confidence in the greatness of God. Although they rarely triumphed over evil in a corporeal sense – they were almost always martyred – they did so through the mass conversions their stoicism and faith made possible. Saints' stories (hagiographies) were so frequently shared and well-known that they could be invoked just by using a symbol to represent them. St Catherine, whose body was broken on a wheel, became synonymous with wheels, while St Sebastian was known by the arrows with which he was martyred. In what might seem to us as a slightly strange twist, medieval people adopted these symbols as their own in their invocation of patron saints. Catherine, for example, was the patron saint of carters: the wheel on which she was tortured became their ever-present symbol of power and devotion as they carted their loads around medieval cities.

To look at a medieval calendar is to be overwhelmed by the sheer number of saints who were venerated in the Middle Ages. Many medieval churches and cathedrals contained relics as a way for their communities to feel closer to God. Everything from fragments of the True Cross, to body parts of the saints, to drops of the Virgin Mary's breast milk was venerated, and often the relics were said to help facilitate miracles. Certain relics and shrines were thought to be more potent than others, which is why people made pilgrimages to places like Canterbury Cathedral, Le Mont Saint-Michel, and Santiago de Compostela. As more and more pilgrims flocked to these shrines, up sprung inns, taverns, and shops featuring everything a traveller might need, much like major vacation spots have today. Churches sold pilgrims' badges as fundraisers for their upkeep, and so pilgrims could bring home a token to remember their journey by (or to show off to their neighbours).

Naturally, there were many more fragments of the True Cross and finger bones of the saints than could ever have come from the real things themselves, and unscrupulous people took advantage of the devoted by selling pigs' bones and bloodied rags as relics. Not everyone was gullible enough to assume that a relic sold on the side of the road was authentic, and the selling and veneration of these false relics was one of the many targets of criticism that the church faced as the Middle Ages drew on. Chaucer's *Canterbury Tales*, for example, features a pardoner who tries to pass off a pillowcase as part of the Virgin Mary's veil among other false relics.

Despite Chaucer's acid pen, however, at the heart of *The Canterbury Tales* is a pilgrimage which even the most cynical characters are undertaking without criticising the actual power of Thomas Becket's shrine to aid them. Medieval people might have smirked at a pardoner selling relics on the road or in the marketplace, but they still believed true relics existed, and didn't doubt those relics' spiritual power.

Did many people go on pilgrimages?

Although there is a common idea that everyone lived and died within the borders of their parishes, medieval people were frequently on the move performing pilgrimages to shrines both near and far. While travelling was expensive, dangerous, and often very long, there were many reasons why a medieval person might undertake a pilgrimage despite these obstacles. Some people wished to gain the aid of a saint whose relic was said to help with a specific problem, such as infertility. Some people wished to give thanks for help that came in an hour of need, or to ask forgiveness for a particularly grievous sin. Some people were fulfilling promises that they'd made in a moment of crisis, and some people were out to perform their devotion by collecting symbols of their journeys in the form of pilgrims' badges.

One of the greatest pilgrimages, of course, was to Jerusalem to visit the holiest places in Christian tradition. While many people hoped to make the trip once in their lifetimes, others were made to go as penance for their sins because a pilgrimage to Jerusalem was no easy task. Not only was it expensive, but it was particularly dangerous given the hostilities between Christians and Muslims in the area, and pilgrims frequently died along the way. Undaunted, they still came in great numbers, and the Templar Order was established to help them get to Jerusalem and back unscathed.

Did everyone believe?

While Christianity pervaded every aspect of daily medieval life, it's important to note that not everyone was faithful, nor did everyone obey the church's rules and ordinances. Then, as now, people's spiritual beliefs were widely varied, but the major difference was that power and religion were much more closely intertwined in the Middle Ages, making dissent unpopular and sometimes dangerous. Doubts about God, and struggles to meet the demands of a good, Christian life were real and heart-breaking.

As we saw in Chapter Three, grief was a moment in which faith could be very fragile, but people were always aware of the difficulties of reconciling the earthly world with the divine. One late medieval song wrestles with fundamental spiritual questions in this way:

> A God and yet a man?
> A maide and yet a mother?
> Wit wonders what wit can
> Conceave [conceive]: this, or the other?
>
> A God – and can he die?
> A dead man – can he live?
> What wit can well replie [reply]?
> What reason reason give?
>
> God, Truth itselfe doth teach it.
> Mans wit senckes [sinks] too far under,
> By reasons power, to reach it.
> Beleeve [believe] and leave to wonder!

While this poet seems relatively content to leave off wondering, Ausiás March, who we met in Chapter Three, agonises over his lack of faith aloud in a poem addressed to God:

> I grieve to see my life draw near its end;
> yet, for all my grief, I cannot love you
> – not as I would: habit is against me
> ... I beg you, Lord, to come into my heart[.]

Beyond private doubts like these, criticism of the church was also widespread and common. Jokes were frequently made about lusty priests and nuns, and well-fed friars. Part of the objection to the church in the Middle Ages – the part which fed into the fat friar stereotype – had to do with its wealth. The church was entitled to one-tenth of the people's income (a tithe) to support its priests and canons who offered masses, advice, and spiritual help in time of need. However, depending on the community, tithing could easily amount to more than could be spent on the wages of the chapter or on the building itself. In addition, people frequently made donations to their local churches as gifts or bequests as a way of atoning for past sins, in thanksgiving for answered prayers, or in hopes of prayers to help them reach heaven. In this way, the church accumulated a whole lot of wealth. While some people were satisfied with their church's ability to buy the best communion plate, hangings, and other items for the sanctuary, others could not help but compare the wealth of the church to the poverty of some of its parishioners.

A second criticism often levelled at the church had to do with its power and exclusivity. For centuries, the Bible was written in Latin, the language of the elite and the clergy, but not of the common people. To attend mass, then, was to hear people speak in a foreign language; only priests and the educated could properly translate the words of God, which meant that a priest was needed in order for people to correctly understand and access divine teachings. Even the prayers which everyone was meant to know, the *Paternoster* ('Our Father'; The Lord's Prayer) and the *Ave Maria* ('Hail, Mary') were not always understood in their entirety by the people reciting them.

This language barrier seemed unfair to the common people, and there was increasing pressure across Europe to translate the Bible into everyday language. In the fourteenth-century, John Wycliffe translated the Bible into English illegally and distributed it. Naturally, he was charged with heresy and executed when he refused to repent. Not all copies of Wycliffe's Bible were destroyed, however; some were hidden away, but people were not to read an official Bible in English for another century and a half.

Wasn't the church always burning people for heresy?

Much is made of medieval intolerance for variation in faith, and incidences of persecution were very real; however, there was more everyday tolerance for beliefs that strayed from the norm than we might have been led to believe.

Because it takes a long time to alter a whole continent's belief system, there were many leftovers from former religions that still existed in Christianised Europe. People frequently believed in faeries and Jesus at the same time, without being burned at the stake for it. Some of the most popular stories of the Middle Ages – the Arthurian legends – frequently combined these pagan ideas with Christianity without issue. For example, Arthur himself is a 'most Christian king', and yet he is conceived through magic, he cavorts with magicians, he rules with a magical sword, and he is taken away to the Otherworld to be healed of his grievous wound. Many people believed Arthur's stories were true, and yet there was no issue with this crossover between Christianity and the Otherworld.

> The days of the week still hearken back to old belief systems, with a combination of Roman and Norse gods: moon's day, Tīw's day, Woden's (Odin's) day, Thor's day, Frigga's day, Saturn's day, and the sun's day.

People who had misguided beliefs were most often gently corrected (more than once) rather than immediately sentenced to death for their error. Faith was somewhat flexible, with room for superstition in and among the teachings of the church. As the centuries passed, it became increasingly inflexible. Although large-scale religious persecution within European communities is commonly thought to be a defining feature of the Middle Ages, it was a relatively late occurrence. The first witch trial was not until the fourteenth century, and the Spanish Inquisition did not begin its work until the fifteenth. The period in which the majority of burnings, hangings, and witch trials occurred was actually the Early Modern Period or Renaissance.

A man bathes at home, risking splinters without a linen sheet to line his bathtub.
(British Library, BL Royal 6 E VI f.179)

A bathhouse offers a convenient place for dinner and other steamy pursuits.
(British Library, BL Royal 17 F IV f.297)

This playful German aquamanile is cast in the shape of a man-eating dragon. (The Met Cloisters)

The Shambles in York, England, offers a glimpse into medieval town life. (Danièle Cybulskie)

As evidence of its fourteenth-century poshness, Doune Castle in Scotland has ensuite garderobes with windows and shelves. (Danièle Cybulskie)

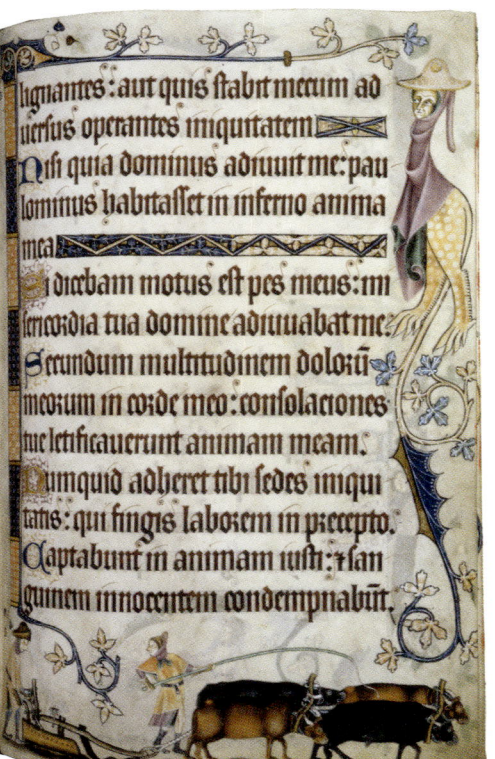

A team of disgruntled peasants guides a plough pulled by oxen in the Luttrell Psalter. (British Library, BL Additional 42130 f.170)

This image from the Luttrell Psalter shows two essential technologies related to medieval food: a watermill, and fish traps. (British Library, BL Additional 42130 f.181)

Caspar (one of the three Magi) is just one of the many people of colour to be found in medieval art. He is dressed in the latest fashion with gold embellishments as befits his station as a king. (The Met Cloisters)

This monk's 'excessive gladness' may mean he'll have some penance assigned to him in the morning. (British Library, BL Sloane 2435 f.44v)

This impressive little boat is a thirteenth-century Parisian saltcellar, made from gold and rock crystal and embellished with precious stones. (The Met Cloisters)

This feast in the Luttrell Psalter features a trestle table, knives and spoons, silver dishes, and a fancy saltcellar. (British Library, BL Additional 42130 f.208)

Although many arranged marriages worked out well, things aren't looking rosy for the couple at this medieval wedding.
(British Library, BL Royal 20 C VII f.182)

Lusty clergy were common figures in medieval jokes and fabliaux.
(British Library, BL Yates Thompson 13 f.177)

This illustration is meant to depict the birth of Alexander the Great, but it shows details from a medieval childbirth: female attendants, warm bedlinens, a fire, and a washtub. (British Library, BL Royal 20 C III f.15)

Although everyone in this miniature seems surprised, dedicating children to be raised and educated by religious communities was a very normal part of medieval life. (British Library, BL Royal 10 D VIII f.82)

A funeral mass is performed by a community of tonsured clergy. (British Library, BL Additional 52539 f.7)

Target practice for archers meant shooting at a 'butt' like these ones. Archery was practised on a weekly basis by every able-bodied man in England in the mid- to late fourteenth century. (British Library, BL Additional 42130 f.147v)

A knight's best friend, weapon, and status symbol was his horse. (British Library, BL Harley 2169 f.3)

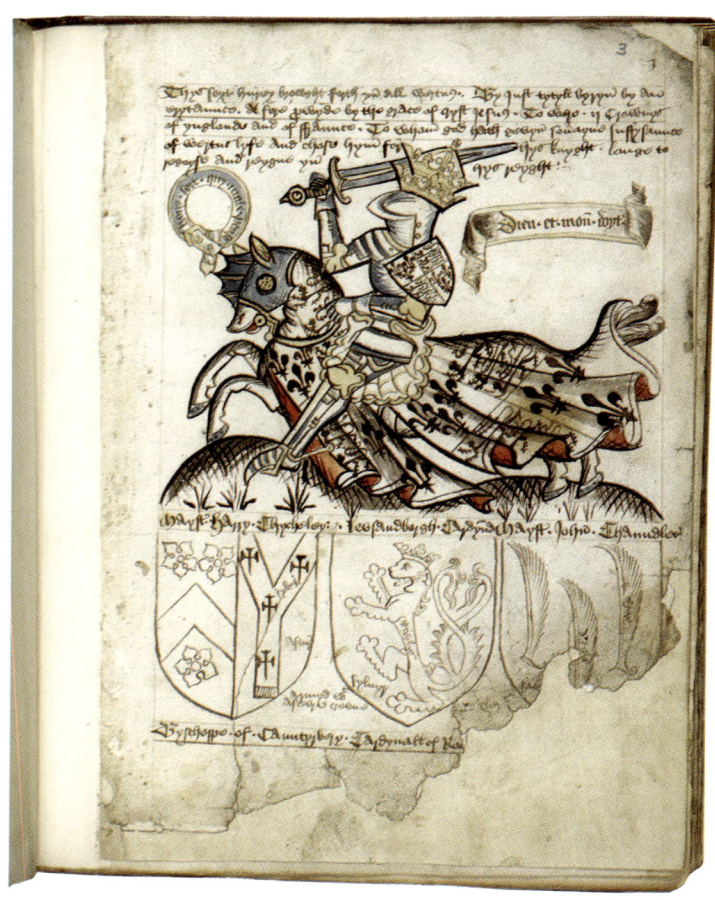

The White Tower at the heart of the Tower of London is the original keep, built shortly after the Norman conquest of 1066 CE. It features square Norman towers, and crenellations at the top of the wall. (Danièle Cybulskie)

The counterweight trebuchet was a fearsome weapon for destroying castle walls or launching nasty surprises into a castle's bailey. (Wikimedia Commons)

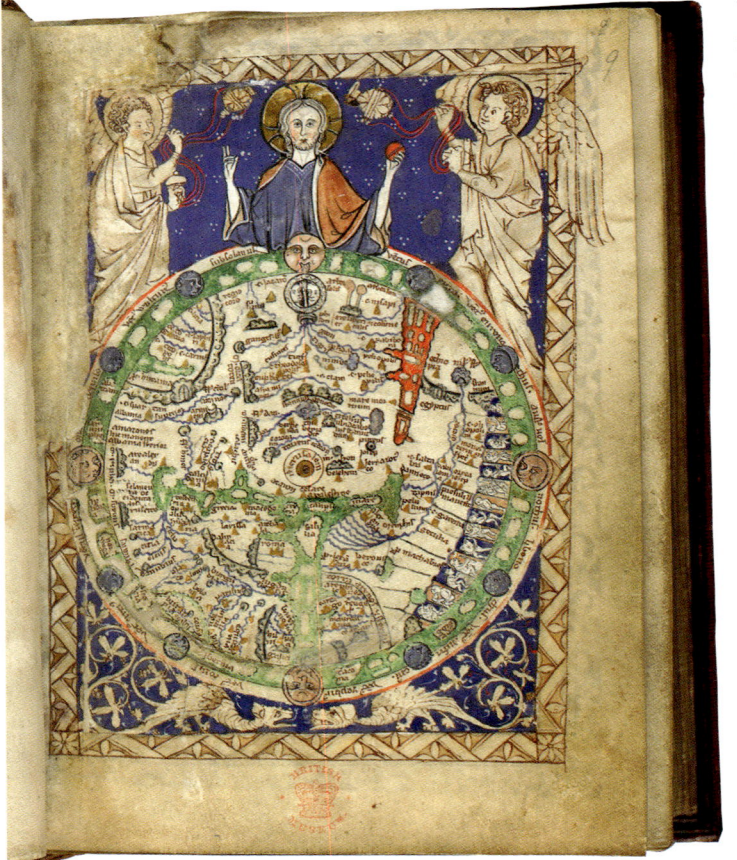

This late medieval siege features longbows, crossbows, guns, and cannons.
(British Library, BL Royal 14 E IV f.23)

Like many European maps, this one features Jesus watching over the globe, with Jerusalem as the centre point of both the Earth and the cosmos.
(British Library, BL Additional 28681 f.9)

Like this one, many monks were given the task of copying books; a long and painstaking process. (British Library, BL Royal 14 E III f. 6v)

One of medieval Europe's most popular saints, St Catherine is represented by the wheel on which she was tortured.
(British Library, BL Additional 24686 f.2v)

This pilgrim's badge depicts the shrine of Thomas Becket at Canterbury Cathedral. The figure at the side is raising the curtain so we can view the shrine.
(The Met Cloisters)

Although medieval Europe is popularly known for religious intolerance, there was wide variation in belief and acceptance. The story of King Arthur is just one of many in which Christianity and pagan ideas integrated seamlessly.
(British Library, BL Additional 10294 f.94)

Family gathers around a patient's bedside as a doctor (right) examines a flask of the patient's urine to diagnosis his illness.
(British Library, BL Harley 4379 f.125v)

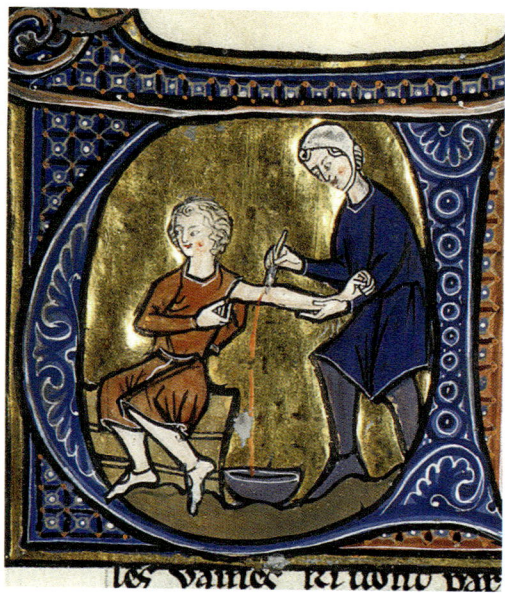

A patient is undergoing bloodletting in order to balance his humours.
(British Library, BL Sloane 2435 f.11v)

As this portrait of 'Old Age' shows, medieval people used various mobility aids like crutches to assist them.
(British Library, BL Harley 4425 f.10v)

Christine De Pizan writes at her desk wearing a *cote hardie* and horned headpiece.
(British Library, BL Harley 4431 f.4)

Women card wool and spin it, using an early spinning wheel.
(British Library, BL Additional 42130 f.193)

This thirteenth-century Scandinavian chess piece features a queen surrounded by a crowd of supplicants. It is made from whale ivory. (The Met Cloisters)

These playing cards from The Met Cloisters feature fashionable figures, from their ermine trim, to the queen's plucked forehead. Their suit features hunting horns, not hearts, diamonds, clubs, or spades. (The Met Cloisters)

The famous fourteenth-century joust at St Inglevert brought together all the most fashionable knights and ladies. The hearts on the knights' shields show just how closely intertwined courtly love and the ideals of chivalry were. (British Library, BL Harley 4379 f.23v)

This bestiary image of a beaver attempts to explain why the beaver's Latin name is 'castor'. (British Library, BL Royal 12 C XIX f.10v)

This is not to say that people were not punished or executed for heresy; they were, but persecutions on a scale such as those of the Cathars and the Templars are remembered because they were shocking, not routine.

What was life like for the Jews?

Anti-Semitism was already firmly established before the rise of Christianity, and, unfortunately, it did not abate during the Middle Ages. Although Jewish communities were closely interconnected with Christian ones in terms of commerce and physical proximity, official regulations continuously sought to keep the two separated as much as possible. Jews were often forbidden to own land and barred from public office. Still, their communities were vibrant, and there are records of Jewish professionals in many different occupations, such as in the case of the doctor who testified at Margarida de Portu's trial (as we saw in Chapter Four). Jews in Aragon even had their own guilds. Some Jews did find themselves as moneylenders to Christians, as Christians were not allowed to loan money at interest. The idea of being indebted to Jews, however, made some Christians extremely resentful.

Because the rituals of Judaism took place mostly behind closed doors – in synagogues or in homes – Christians were not privy to the goings on, making the mystery of Jewish religious practices another convenient breeding ground for anti-Semitic speculation. This perfect storm of resentment and ignorance simmered quietly most of the time, erupting into horrific violence when triggered by outside events.

As we've seen with mixed bathing, there was a constant worry that a person might accidentally form friendships or fall in love or lust across religious lines. Since it was all too easy to form this kind of human bond with neighbours of a different faith, Innocent III required that all Jews and 'Saracens' (Muslims) be required to wear distinctive dress in order to avoid unwitting contact, especially sexual contact. For the Jews, this distinctive article of clothing was clarified in 1227 CE to be 'an oval badge, the measure of one finger in width and one half a palm in height' to be worn on the chest, much like the yellow Star of David in Nazi Germany.

Although Jews were ostensibly under the protection of their kings, in reality, kings were notably absent when push came to shove, and exploited their Jewish citizens when it suited them. Three generations of English kings (John, Henry III, and Edward I) mercilessly taxed, imprisoned, and harassed England's Jewish population before Edward expelled the Jews altogether in 1290 CE, confiscating the rest of their money and goods. Philip the Fair of France followed suit less than two decades later, expelling the Jews from his own country, and likewise keeping their assets. Ferdinand of Aragon and Isabella of Castile did the same, expelling the Jews (and Muslims) from their newly united Spain in 1492 CE.

As religious 'outsiders', the Jews were extremely vulnerable to scapegoating, especially in times of upheaval. Lies were spread about Jews ritually murdering children as part of their religious practice, and during the Black Death Jews were accused of poisoning wells to bring on the pestilence. Pogroms occurred all over Europe.

While everyday life most often saw Jews and Christians knowing and relating to each other on a human level, in good ways and in bad, a sword of Damocles was forever hanging over the heads of the Jews; an ever-present spectre of violence, ready to suddenly mete out destruction at the hands of yesterday's friends.

What about Muslims?

Islam was born in the Middle Ages along with the Prophet Mohammed in the Middle East in the sixth century. Belief spread rapidly along the Silk Road, and Islam quickly established itself as a major religion, as important and influential as Judaism and Christianity.

Because Islam has its roots in these earlier religions, the same sites which were (and are) considered holy to Jews and Christians were (and are) considered holy to Muslims, especially Jerusalem. This, of course, led to Christians and Muslims fighting for possession of the city, as believers on both sides wished to control both the holy sites and this nexus of trade between Europe, Asia, and Africa.

Although the period that followed the Middle Ages was called the 'Renaissance' ('rebirth') after the 'rediscovery' of classical texts from Ancient Greece and Rome, in reality, these texts were never actually lost. While they fell into disuse by Christians during the Early Middle Ages, they were in continuous translation and use by Muslims throughout the Middle Ages. In fact, many of the 'rediscovered' texts were rediscovered by Christians not directly from Greek or Latin, but through Muslim translation and transmission.

Islamic thinkers were the frontrunners of science during this period, with discoveries about mathematics, technology, and medicine often outstripping their Christian counterparts. Scholars at universities studied the medical texts of doctors such as Avicenna to learn about treatments, while Muslim astronomers made complex calculations about the heavens, continuously adding to their knowledge and improving upon devices such as the astrolabe. Although they may not have had a generous word to say about Islamic beliefs, medieval Christians could not deny the superiority of Muslim knowledge in many subjects, and wisely adopted their ideas.

The hatred between Christians and Muslims was at its most intense in the Holy Land, where the stakes were high and people were being slaughtered. This didn't mean, however, that people couldn't act civilly towards each other when they chose to, or that they didn't form alliances when it suited them. When the Mamluks threatened the Holy Land, Muslims and Christians swore to fight together to defeat this new threat. In the event, they never did, but their willingness to shake hands shows that (as with medieval Christians and Jews) human relations across religious lines are much more complex than the broad strokes of history might suggest.

What about the crusades?

In theory, the crusades were about the capture of Jerusalem for Christianity, so that it was in the 'rightful' hands of the Christian people and available for pilgrims to visit the holy sites. In reality, the crusades were a messy business that included fighting against Muslims in the Holy Land, modern Spain, and Portugal, as well as fighting against heretics in southern France (and also some unsanctioned looting of Christian Byzantium).

The 'First Crusade' to capture Jerusalem was preached in the late eleventh century by Pope Urban II, and the idea took off like wildfire. The Muslims were surprised by this sudden collective outbreak of hostilities, and Jerusalem fell to the Christians in 1099 CE. The vast number of Christian pilgrims who came flocking to this dangerous hotspot in the aftermath was what inspired the establishment of the Templar Order, a protective force dedicated to keeping pilgrims safe. The Most Venerable Order of the Hospital of St John of Jerusalem (known as the Hospitallers) was another formidable military order formed in the Holy Land, and despite its commitment to the Christian faith, treated Muslims and Jews as well as Christians at its namesake hospital. Unlike the Templars, whose order was utterly destroyed in the fourteenth century, the Hospitallers are still in existence today as the Knights of Malta.

As soon as the Christians had established themselves in the Holy Land, they began squabbling over it, with poor leadership and decision-making. In the meantime, a new power was rising in the form of Ṣalāḥ al-Dīn Yūsuf ibn Ayyūb – known to Christians as Saladin. Saladin was consolidating Muslim power in the Middle East as the Christians were arguing among themselves, and when the Christian forces rode out against his army at the Battle of Hattin, they were wiped out, clearing the way for Saladin to take Jerusalem in 1187 CE.

The fall of Jerusalem was horrifying to European Christians, and they immediately set out to get it back (this was the 'Third Crusade'). Some of the most famous kings of the Middle Ages – Richard I (The Lionheart) of England, Philip II (Augustus) of France, and Frederick Barbarossa of the Holy Roman Empire (based mainly in modern Germany) – all headed for the Holy Land to face down Saladin. Things did not go as planned, as Frederick Barbarossa drowned along the way, Richard and Philip only managed to take Acre and Jaffa (not Jerusalem), and Richard was captured and imprisoned on the way home while Philip plotted his overthrow with his treacherous brother, John. Still, it was a relative success in that Richard managed to come to an agreement with Saladin that Christians would be safely allowed to visit Jerusalem despite the general hostilities. This was the last real success Christian crusaders would have in the Holy Land.

After the Third Crusade, there were several more efforts; however, none of them managed to recapture Jerusalem, and the Christians were gradually squeezed out of the Holy Land altogether by the Muslims and then the Mamluks. The fall of Acre in 1291 CE was a humiliating moment for the crusaders, and (unbeknownst to them as they sailed away in grief) the death knell for the Templars.

Alongside all the turmoil in the Holy Land, crusades were being preached and fought in Europe, as well. Not only were Christians encouraged to fight to conquer Muslim Spain in a long drawn out effort now known as the *Reconquista*, but they were also charged with fighting heretics in France. As crusader efforts were failing in the Middle East, they were succeeding little by little in Iberia, where Christian kingdoms were established in Castile, Aragon, and Navarre by 1250 CE. As we've seen, it was the marriage and combined forces of Isabella and Ferdinand which led to the capture of Granada, completing the *Reconquista* in 1492 CE.

The crusade in the south of France was preached by Innocent III, who was alarmed by the spread of Catharism, a heresy which involved the binary forces of good and evil, but rejected Catholic teachings, such as the humanity of Jesus. Considering it was a heretical belief, Catharism was popular, even among the nobility. The same military tactics used by crusaders in the Middle East were used against the Cathars, including siege, sacking, and mass slaughter. This was the beginning of the Inquisition, spearheaded by Dominican friars, that was to gain such a fearsome reputation in the Late Middle Ages.

No group of people came out of the crusades innocent (not even Innocent, himself). Massacres occurred on both sides of the dividing lines, even by those who have gone down in history as heroes: Saladin, a man praised for his courtesy, killed every one of the Templars he captured at Hattin, and Richard, that legend of English history, killed thousands of hostages at Acre. Appalling things were done in the name of religion and hatred.

This 'Age of Faith' was a dramatic time for Europe, in which the pervasiveness of Christianity in everything from the food on the table to the church bells ringing the canonical hours regularly stirred unearthly bliss in the true believer, tormented doubts in the sceptic, and deep unease in the hearts of those who were not of the dominant faith. People did their best to follow the tenets of their faith, even while harbouring suspicions that there were faeries in the woods just beyond the borders of their lands. Underneath the sweeping statements of popes and kings as to what the faithful were meant to do and believe lies the other story of faith in the Middle Ages: that of the countless Christians (orthodox and heretic), Muslims, and Jews who quietly lived and worked together in peace and compassion across Europe and the Middle East while intolerance rained around them.

Chapter Six

In Sickness and in Health

Medieval medicine has a bad reputation for being little more than wishful thinking and bloodletting. If this was the extent of it, however, no one at all would have survived either the battles or the corporal punishments we looked at in Chapter Four. The truth is that while bloodletting was indeed a popular treatment, medieval medical practitioners knew much more about how to deal with everyday ailments than just where people's veins were.

There's evidence to suggest that not only did medieval people have a wide range of options available to them when it came to their health, but also that some of their treatments would have worked pretty well. That said, there are still plenty of reasons to be grateful for twenty-first-century healthcare.

What happened when people got hurt?

If someone was injured, there was first aid to be had. Of the modern first-aid formula RICE – rest, ice, compression, elevation – the only thing medieval Europeans might not have applied was ice; unless it was the middle of winter, that is.

Modern antiseptic wasn't available, but people knew enough to wash a dirty wound before bandaging it, especially with alcohol. Bleeding cuts could be packed with spiderwebs, moss, and honey. While all of these may sound like terrible ideas, they actually worked remarkably well. Spiderwebs and honey are sticky enough to help hold the cut together, and moss is absorbent, keeping linen bandages from soaking through too quickly. On top of those obvious qualities, both honey and the moulds that grow in some mosses have antibacterial properties.

These remedies would have kept wounds both moist and clean. Deep cuts could be sutured with silk thread or cauterised.

For burns, there was snail slime, or ointments made from mulberry leaves, or a mixture of apple, wine, wax, tallow, mastic and frankincense. Sunburns could be treated with an ointment of lily root, white lead, mastic, frankincense, camphor, tallow, and rose water, as *The Trotula* suggests. Unfortunately, lead is poisonous, but at least your sunburn won't hurt as much.

For mild pain relief, there was white willow bark to chew or drink as a tea. Like honey, this remedy would really have worked, too, as willow bark contains salicylic acid/salicin, which a close relative of something we still stock in our medicine cabinets today: acetylsalicylic acid, better known as aspirin. Stronger painkillers would be used for surgery (see below). If the willow bark didn't cut it, there was always alcohol.

Because many treatments, like using splints and tourniquets, are both simple and common sense, people didn't feel the need to include them in books, unlike herbal remedies which required more careful preparation and dosages. This may be disappointing to historians who would like every detail recorded, but then again, we don't tend to include simple procedures like splinter removal in our first aid books, either.

What happened when people got sick?

Medieval people didn't have a clear concept of germs, nor did they have modern sterilisation processes or antibiotics, so it's no wonder they frequently got sick. If a person did fall ill, the first recourse was prayer, either formally, using established words, or informally, the way people still tend to say, 'please, don't let me be sick', when we're sure we're coming down with something at an inconvenient moment.

Much of medieval healthcare involved a remedy along with a prayer, so even if someone was using medicine, faith was still very much a part of the treatment. For example, a prayer to the actual herbs used in medicine has been found in several manuscripts from as early as the sixth century, to as late as the thirteenth:

> Come hither with your powers, because he who created you has given me leave to gather you; he also to whom medicine is entrusted shows his favor [sic]. As much as is in your power, grant good medicine for the sake of health. I implore you, bestow favor on me through your protection, that whatever I make from you with all your powers, and to whomever I give [this medicine], it may have a most speedy effect and a good outcome.

For those with chronic illnesses, more drastic action might be necessary. In these cases, offerings might be made to the church in the form of votives (wax figures of the afflicted body part); donations of items the church needed, like candles, cloth, or dishes; or items that were important to the donor.

Pilgrimage was another way in which people could ask for spiritual aid to help them with their physical ailments. To become a saint, a person had to have performed miracles either while alive or after death, and many of these saintly miracles were medical ones in which the saint healed conditions such as paralysis, blindness, or deafness. To access the healing properties of saints, it was usually necessary to visit their shrines and venerate – or even touch – their relics. A wealthy person could also bring home a relic, such as a vial with a drop of a martyr's blood, to use as a healing aid.

Did they rely solely on faith?

No. Although the faithful believed that no healing would occur without God being involved, they did not rely solely on him to save them. In fact, relying too much on God's help for earthly troubles was considered foolish.

If you knew what you needed, or just needed a simple remedy, you would visit the local apothecary shop. There, you could get the ingredients you needed so that you could put the remedy together yourself, or you could get premade mixtures, creams, and ointments. Many medicinal ingredients were also culinary, which meant that the apothecary shop was also where you could pick up the imported spices you might need for cooking, like cinnamon, cumin, and ginger. As we saw in Chapter One, the natural spices and powders that could be found at the apothecary shop could also be used for beauty and grooming products like deodorant and tooth powder.

The very same spices, powders, and mixing methods that were used in medieval medicine and cosmetics were useful in making pigments, too, so apothecaries also sold ink. This saved scribes and illuminators who could afford it the trouble of making their own inks, and the apothecary's long practice and skill with mixtures gave them a better chance at having regular colours and consistency, as well. As a complementary skill, apothecaries' proficiency with wax as a binding and mixing agent led them to create and sell wax products alongside their other wares, such as candles, votives (as seen above), and sealing wax. The combination of ink and sealing wax made it a logical step for apothecaries to sell parchment, and other stationery items, too. Our modern habit of heading to the pharmacy for a headache cure, grooming products, and stationery is part of a long tradition, indeed.

What if they needed surgery?

While there were hospitals in the Middle Ages, they were more focused on providing long-term care for the poor and chronically ill than emergency services (think 'hospitality'). Gradually, the emphasis became more firmly placed on medicine, but for surgery, people took a different route.

Although it may seem ludicrous to entrust your health care to the person who trims your hair, that is exactly what medieval people did when they needed surgery: they saw the barber-surgeon. It does make a certain amount of sense, however, as the same two things are needed for both shaving and surgery: a steady hand, and an extremely sharp knife. The very idea of medieval surgery probably brings to mind the most gruesome images, and it's true that the surgical environment left much to be desired by modern standards. However, surgery in the Middle Ages was a lot more sophisticated than we tend to give medieval people credit for.

The most frequent surgery was amputation, as accidents and warfare combined with the lack of antibiotics meant that gangrene was always a risk. Richard the Lionheart, himself, died of an infected wound having been shot in the shoulder while foolishly parading around within crossbow range of a French castle he was besieging. Sometimes, wounds were kept clean of gangrene through the use of maggots, which will eat dead flesh but not living flesh, thereby preventing any decay from festering within the wound. Modern science has now returned to this practice in some cases to similarly prevent the need for amputation of limbs.

Possibly one of the worst aspects of medieval life, amputation could be a slow process that (like other medieval surgeries) had to be performed without modern anaesthesia, although patients could be well-lubricated with alcohol or given drugs such as willow bark, or – even better – opium. Avicenna also recommends 'mandrake (and its seeds and bark of its root), poppy plants, henbane, black nightshade, and lettuce seeds'. Naturally, you'd want the expertise of a master apothecary to measure enough nightshade to put you to sleep temporarily, not permanently.

Once the surgery was completed, the wound could be cauterised to close it up, stop the bleeding, and speed healing. Avicenna says, 'The best material to use for cauterisation is gold,' but it's unlikely that most people had access to such posh equipment. Although he goes in-depth into the methods of cautery, suffice it to say that the cauterisation should produce 'a deep and thick scab that does not fall off quickly.' Suturing was also a possibility if the surgical site was tricky or involved internal organs, like caesarean section.

In addition to cutting your hair and removing troublesome limbs, barber-surgeons were also responsible for tooth-pulling and bloodletting. For the best advice on when and how to get yourself bled, however, you'd see an actual medical doctor.

Did they have doctors like we do today?

Sort of. Medical doctors in the Middle Ages were people who, like today, finished their basic schooling and then went off to specialised universities, the most prestigious of which were in the Italian cities of Bologna and Salerno. Because the church did not permit autopsies, and technology like microscopes did not exist, medical knowledge was acquired through the observation of the outer body and by studying Greek, Roman, and Muslim texts. As a result, the treatments of a medieval doctor were more philosophical and holistic than the straightforward ministrations of the barber-surgeon.

Medieval doctors believed that physical health – as well as mental health – is based on the balance of four humours, or fluids, within the body: blood, phlegm, yellow bile, and black bile. Each of these humours also corresponds to a condition: wet, dry, hot, and cold. If your humours were out of balance, you could rebalance them by eating the correct foods or being subjected to the right environmental conditions, usually the opposite of what you had in excess. So, if you were suffering from a condition that indicated you had too much blood or phlegm in your body, you could balance out your humours by eating something dry.

If simple interventions weren't enough to fix the problem, doctors could siphon off some of the excess humours in the form of bloodletting. Leeches could be used to remove blood from the patient, or doctors (or barber-surgeons) could also make a small cut to drain the excess blood into a bowl in the more familiar image. They could also perform cupping: applying heated bowls to the skin.

> Leeches were used often enough in medieval medical treatments that the Anglo-Saxon word for doctor was *læce*. Leeches are still used in Western medicine today, and are registered – along with maggots – as living medical devices.

Medieval doctors were unlike like those we have today as they were also trained in arts which modern Western people might not associate with medicine, such as astronomy and astrology. Because it was believed that the stars and planets influenced our physical and mental health day to day, it was critical for doctors to know the right phase of the moon or conjunction of planets in order to better help their patients.

What about women's medicine?

Unfortunately, women themselves were increasingly shoved out of the medical profession, and generally not permitted to be doctors, as they were not allowed to attend university. There were a few exceptions, and it seems likely that doctors' wives and daughters would also have picked up medical skills while assisting at home. While medical books did have information on women's health and medicine, it's relatively sparse.

The Trotula, a compilation of several people's knowledge from the university town of Salerno, is probably the best and most specific collection of knowledge of women's medicine, though it also contains sections on cosmetics and grooming (as we saw in Chapter One). The spread of the existing copies suggests that *The Trotula* was widely read all over Europe, especially in universities. It covers a range of information which would have been especially useful to doctors (men) who would rarely or never have attended a birth or dealt with a stillbirth under normal circumstances but its bad advice on contraception (for example, carrying around dried weasel testicles) suggests that even this specialised book was probably not where women tended to get all their vital information.

Medical doctors had been trained by the church, so while they might have been happy to provide advice on fertility, reproductive issues such as contraception and abortion presented them with a conflict of interest. Instead, women could do what they have for generations: call the midwife. It goes without saying that midwives had a hugely important function in society, and while they were paid to support women during birth, by extension midwives were also knowledgeable about fertility, contraception, abortion, lactation, and problematic periods. Their connection with herbal lore, sexuality, and fertility (and its reverse) was part of the reason they were so targeted during late medieval and Early Modern witch trials. Midwives knew what to advise women *not* to eat while they were pregnant, for example, which means they knew *why* not.

What about people with disabilities?

Without the benefit of modern technology, life for medieval people with disabilities could sometimes be difficult and isolating. That doesn't mean, however, that we should assume there was no quality of life or compassion. When people with disabilities needed extra help, families, communities, clergy, and even lawmakers are known to have looked out for their welfare. It's true that European culture was definitely ableist, but medieval attitudes towards disability varied.

Since medieval Europe was at war fairly frequently, there were always people with visible physical disabilities, whether from conflict, accident, disease, or genetics. Manuscript images show people using mobility aids, such as carts and crutches, and even simple prostheses in the form of wooden legs. One medieval soldier even had an iron hand cast for himself to replace the one that had been amputated, although the expense (and the sheer cumbersome nature of an iron prosthesis) would not have made this practical for most people.

Hearing loss was not uncommon, but unfortunately there were no hearing aids beyond cupping the ear for amplification. Profound deafness was more of a challenge than it is today in that there were no standardised sign languages (beyond the simple gestures used by monks and nuns under vows of silence) and literacy rates were low, so writing down information to communicate wasn't always an option. As deaf people today know, you can make yourself understood in the hearing world much of the time just by using gestures or pictures, although this can be tremendously slow and frustrating. Because of the lack of common language, deaf culture as we know it today did not exist.

Blindness was a similarly common condition. From the thirteenth century onwards, people with poor or fading vision could use glasses, if they could afford them, but these were more like general magnifying glasses than the personalised lenses we have today; enlarging things that were close, not compensating for poor distance vision. Just like they do in the modern world, the visually impaired navigated by sound and touch, sometimes using canes or service dogs to interpret the landscape in front of them. In some places, like Paris, dedicated hospitals for the blind cared for people who could not live on their own.

Cognitive impairment and mental illness were also known in the Middle Ages, and medieval people accepted that someone who had recently returned from war or had received a devastating head wound was likely to experience changes in his personality or ability. Legal contingency plans were in place, created in the wake of powerful men returning from war changed, either through (what we'd now call) acquired brain injuries or post-traumatic stress disorder. Medieval laws in these cases and in cases of congenital cognitive impairment distinguished mainly between whether or not these disabilities were temporary or permanent. If the change looked to be temporary, a guardian was appointed to care for the person and his or her property until the person was functioning as they had before. If permanent, their care would be entrusted to a guardian permanently, and no big decisions were to be made about their property until the disabled person died and it came into the hands of his or her heir.

What might be surprising to modern people is that medieval law recognised that people with cognitive disabilities or mental illness did not have the capacity for evil intent when it came to crime. Most often, they were found to be not legally responsible – even for murder – and they were not punished, though they might be confined for the safety of the community. Interestingly, one of the ways in which people ascertained whether or not the accused was criminally responsible was the way he or she acted after the crime. People who tried to cover up what they'd done were believed to have recognised the difference between right and wrong. The same argument can be seen in use today in court hearings regarding an accused's fitness to stand trial. Repeat offenders, no matter what their capacity, however, were still at risk of the gallows.

Not everyone was kind and understanding towards people with disabilities and, much like today, the disabled could be abused and taken advantage of, especially if they were reduced to begging or homelessness in cities. Sometimes, the methods used to keep people from hurting themselves or others were ones that we would find cruel, such as restraint or long-term confinement in relative isolation. The language used to describe disabilities, like 'idiot' for someone with a cognitive impairment or learning disability, is harsh to our ears, and it was not taboo for disabled people to be the be the butt of jokes. Since some people were mutilated as part of judicial punishments, discrimination in the form of prejudice was another obstacle that disabled people had to face, as someone missing a hand, for example, might be automatically assumed to be a thief. Finally, because accessibility was not paramount – or even normalised – in medieval culture, concerns about safety and discrimination made it extra-challenging for people with disabilities to travel far from home.

All that said, people with disabilities tended to be known within their communities, and the nature of their disabilities and necessary care would also have been known and understood within those communities on an individual level. This meant that the people around them could choose to be kind or cruel based on a huge number of factors, human decency being a large part of the equation.

What was the Black Death?

The Black Death was a vast outbreak of disease that affected populations across Europe, Asia, the Middle East, and Africa from 1347–1349 CE. It's believed to have been a combination of bubonic and pneumonic plague from the bacterium *Yersinia pestis*, spread through flea bites, coughing, and sneezing. Symptoms were a high fever, and telltale black buboes (swellings) in the lymph nodes at the armpits and groin.

The Black Death killed at an incredibly fast rate. The amount of time from the appearance of the first symptoms to the time of death was sometimes as short as twenty-four hours. In just over one year, Europe had lost 30–60 per cent of its entire population. Millions upon millions of people were dead. At the time, it wasn't called 'The Black Death': it was simply called 'the pestilence', or sometimes 'The Great Mortality'. Understandably, people thought it was the end of the world.

Though people tried herbal remedies, prayer, and quarantine, the Black Death was simply too virulent to be controlled. It returned again in 1361 CE, and at intervals throughout the medieval and Early Modern periods. In fairness to medieval doctors, no one was able to effectively combat this plague until the twentieth century, when the advent of antibiotics meant that *Y. pestis* could be controlled.

As brilliant as medieval medical practitioners could be, the Black Death is possibly the single biggest reason to be grateful for nearly 700 more years of medical research. Still, more was known about medicine than the devastation caused by this disease would suggest. Medieval skeletons frequently show that people healed from injuries, illness, and surgeries, and that is thanks to the doctors, apothecaries, barber-surgeons, midwives, and local healers who stepped up to the bedside or the battlefield to save lives in the best way they knew how. Their study – especially of the natural world – has proven invaluable, not only to the lives of those they saved, but to those of their children's children, some of whom are no doubt reading these words.

Chapter Seven

Couture, Competition, and Courtly Love

While it's true that medieval life could be difficult, with long hours and lean times, not every moment was filled with work and worry. People indulged themselves in the latest fashions and fads, and they spent holidays and long winter nights with music and games. Fashion, music, flirtation, and competition all came together at the impressive spectacle that was the tournament, rightly remembered as a wonder of the medieval world. Quieter moments were passed reading tales of Camelot out of lushly illuminated manuscripts, or listening to a troubadour sing of love and heartache.

What medieval people did with their leisure time, talent, and energy tells us just as much about them as how they made ends meet, and they spent it making the most out of life, from the way they dressed to the stories they told.

What did people wear?

Medieval people wore endless variations of the same style of garment: a long-sleeved, T-shaped piece of clothing that went over the head. Men wore shorter, tunic-style versions, while women wore a longer, dress-like style. Linen chemises were worn close to the skin, with woollen outer garments for warmth, modesty, and fashion. Men tended to wear leggings or hose that were two pieces, tied at the top or gartered at the knee, and women wore stockings that didn't go up quite as high. Everyone wore shoes except for the most pious Franciscan monks, and hats for both practical reasons and modesty. From here, the fashions grew and changed.

Gowns were some of the medieval person's most prized possessions. They were the outermost garment, usually worn long for both men and women, and as rich as a person's rank and coin purse permitted. Gowns could be trimmed or lined with fur for warmth, slashed to show just how much expensive material was used in their making, and either loose or form-fitting. They were not only status symbols for the rich, however: they were also markers of intellectual status. Doctors (the PhD kind and the MD kind) wore scarlet gowns, although different schools and universities chose their own colours later in the Middle Ages.

The biggest changes in fashion started happening when tailors started aiming for a closer silhouette. This could be achieved through lacing at the sides or sleeves, or by using a brand-new thirteenth-century invention: buttons. Before the invention of buttons, laces and brooches were the main way of keeping your clothing on; buttons allowed for tighter, more form-fitting fashions. In the fourteenth century, trendy designers showed off shoulders and cleavage with the tight bodice of the *cote hardie*, while the more modest sorts of men and women covered up from the neck down with high-collared *houppelandes*. From the neck down to the buttocks, that is, where noblemen showed off their assets in new, form-fitting two-legged hose. (Women kept theirs modestly covered up.)

> Ladies' sleeves were often detachable in the later Middle Ages, so that women could change their style without having to commission or create an entirely new gown. These sleeves could also be given as 'favours' for knights in tournaments to wear as a token of their ladies' love and esteem.

The fourteenth-century also saw its nobles showing off how much material they could afford. Hats, sleeves, and shoes all grew longer and longer to the point of impracticality. In fact, impracticality *was* the point: the people who wore such fashions were showing off the fact that they didn't really have to work for a living. The pointed princess hats in today's children's costume-sets are a throwback to this fashion.

Beyond just pointed cones, ladies wore both elaborate hairstyles and sculpted hats. Young, unmarried women and girls wore their hair loose as a symbol of their maidenhood, but married women kept their heads covered. Fashions ranged from full, opaque veils, hoods, and hats in the shape of horns, to braids wrapped around the head or over the ears (like a certain beloved sci-fi princess) and covered with a fine, mesh veil and a fillet: a headband which kept the veil in place. Medieval wimples, which modestly covered the head and chin and were topped by a veil, are still worn today by nuns. Women also wore makeup and plucked their eyebrows and foreheads, although this last dangerous vanity could later be punished by demons with hot needles according to at least one medieval sermon.

People in medieval Europe were very keen to establish who everyone was and what their position was at a glance. After all, this would tell them who it was correct to speak with, smile at, or share a drink with. Not only did people give advice on how to dress their parts, but actual laws were also enacted in order to ensure that status was always evident. These laws, called sumptuary laws, restricted everything from dyes, to furs, to fabrics, and like those enacted by Edward III in 1363 CE, were meant to stop upstart citizens who had become wealthier since the Black Death from dressing like their betters, 'violating their estate and degree, to the great destruction of the whole land' through their 'outrageous and excessive apparel'.

Did they wear accessories?

Yes. Because of the expense and the difficulty of making clothing, it was easier for medieval people to change their style by simply switching out accessories – if they could afford them.

In medieval Europe, everyone wore belts or girdles. Not only did they give the figure a fashionable silhouette, but they were also immensely practical in an era in which people didn't normally have pockets sewn into their clothing. From their belts, people hung the things to which they needed ready access, such as keys, eating knives, coin purses, and even (in the case of noble ladies) prayer books. Men, of course, wore sword belts, too.

Like modern people, medieval people wore earrings, rings, necklaces, and bracelets. Naturally, those who could afford jewellery made with precious metals or precious stones, did. People who were not as flush with cash wore glass beads, coloured ribbons, and wooden pendants. Beautifully-coloured enamel rivalled precious stones for colour and shine.

Signet rings were worn by everybody and anybody who had even a moderate amount of success, wealth, or standing. They were used to press into hot sealing wax to let the receiver of a document know who had sent it. Signet rings were therefore carved with a symbol which represented the wearer, whether it was the badge of their family, or their own personal insignia. They were a smaller version of the great seals which kings and popes used to endorse decrees and laws instead of writing their signatures.

How did people make their clothes?

Most of the fabric in used in the Middle Ages was broadcloth, wool woven into a standard size of '26 to 28 yards long and 1 ¾ yards wide'. Wool had to be shorn from sheep; carded or combed; washed; spun; dyed or bleached; woven; fulled; napped; and pressed. Linen followed a similar pattern, except that the fibres were harvested from flax. Silk threads from Asia could be combined with these other fibres to create a variety of fabrics of variable weight and luxury.

Yarn which was spun at home was usually spun on a drop spindle: a short stick with a circular weight at the end. The spinner started high up, giving the spindle a quick twist to get it spinning while feeding the fibres through her fingers. The fibres twisted into thread or yarn as the spindle made its way down to the floor (hence, 'drop'). Medieval women would have been trained to do this from girlhood, with girls who were too young to spin carding the wool and watching their elders.

The other method for spinning was using a wheel, invented in the late twelfth century. Manuscript images of these spinning wheels, such as can be found in the Luttrell Psalter, show that they don't differ much from those used all the way up until the Industrial Revolution, and still in use today. Initially, spinning wheels were turned by hand or by sticks, but in the fifteenth century the treadle spinning wheel was invented, hugely increasing productivity. Drop spindles were much cheaper and easier to make, however, and they remained in use.

Dyeing required gathering many different materials from the natural world and boiling the yarn or cloth in them. This process was dependent on international trade, as some of the most desirable dyes required very specific materials. Red dye, for example, required crushed kermes, an insect not found in northern Europe, while alum, found in Asia, was required to set dyes. Because dyeing required exotic supplies, extra time, and therefore extra expense, the poorest and most pious people would skip this step, wearing undyed wool clothing in the natural blacks, browns, greys, and whites of sheep.

After the yarn was spun (and perhaps dyed), it needed to be woven. People had been using vertical looms since antiquity, with stones or weights holding down the warp (vertical strands) while a person standing up wove a shuttle across to create the weft (horizontal strands). In the thirteenth century, the horizontal loom was invented, which allowed the weaver to sit and run the shuttle across. As with the spinning wheel, manuscript images show that the horizontal loom has likewise not changed much in centuries. Weaving could be, and was, done at home by women, although the professional weavers tended to be men. A broadcloth loom was a two-man operation because it was so wide; one person pushed the shuttle across the warp threads while the other caught it at the other end. Linen looms were not as broad, and therefore possible to operate single-handedly. This was useful because it meant that linen undergarments, towels, napkins, and bedlinens could all be made at home, so long as a household was able to afford the necessary tools.

Once the broadcloth was woven, it had to be fulled to tighten the weave. This was often done by trampling the cloth underfoot in a mixture of water and urine, although later in the Middle Ages, fulling mills were invented to hammer the cloth using waterpower. Then it was napped to remove all of the fluffy bits, and finally pressed.

Because cloth was so costly and took so much effort to make, clothing wasn't usually pre-made and sold off the rack, but was custom-tailored to fit. (There was a bustling second-hand clothing trade, however). Tailoring could be done at home or by a professional, and as with other textile work, the work done at home was usually by women, while the professional work was usually done by men. As with so many other medieval professions, a weaver, dyer, or tailor would often have women working in the workshop, but in most places, these women were not permitted to become masters, themselves.

Once a piece of clothing was patterned and cut, it was ready to be sewn together and embellished. Even royal ladies sewed and embroidered clothing for their families and elaborate textiles for the church. Since this was a time before the rise of machines and mass-production, every needle used was made by hand out of bone, ivory, metal, or wood so they were much more valuable to their owners than today's throwaway needles.

The rich, the higher clergy, and the royals wore clothing embellished with thread made of precious metals, or with gemstones. Gold and silver thread was made by wrapping fine filaments of metal around a core thread – painstaking work. Paintings of medieval royalty show massive amounts of gold thread in use, as well as precious stones from all over the world. These elaborate and costly embellishments sometimes made clothing quite heavy and hot to wear, but it was worth it for the sake of fashion and royal splendour.

Did medieval people wear underwear?

Yes, it seems that some people did. Even St Benedict required his monks to borrow a pair of communal underwear if they were going on a long trip outside the walls, and to return them after they were washed. These were likely to have been long shorts or 'breeches' rather than the briefs we may picture. Over the years, men's breeches got shorter and tighter, more like today's boxers, and they even had a fly for convenience.

An unexpected trove of fifteenth-century textiles discovered in Austria contained not only a fully intact pair of underwear that resemble today's string-bikini style, but also four garments that have turned out to be the oldest known brassieres. All of these pieces were made of linen, unsurprisingly, and the bras have tailored cups meant to support the breasts rather than bind them. No evidence of chainmail bikinis has ever been found.

What did they do for fun?

Although Europeans were expected to go to church whenever possible, a more entertaining way for them to learn the Christian story was by watching plays. Religious plays were called 'mystery' plays, as they revealed the mysteries of God's work as written in the Bible. Some of these are 'cycle' plays, as they go through the cycle of human history on Earth as shown through a Christian lens. The York cycle is the biggest one that survives, with forty-eight short pageants meant to be performed over the course of a day.

What's fascinating about mystery plays and cycle plays is that, unlike in the periods both before and after the Middle Ages, they weren't performed by professional actors. Rather, members of the community would take on the roles, with each of the tradesmen's guilds being assigned the pageant which seemed most appropriate in a practical sense; for example, the shipbuilders' guild would perform the Noah's ark pageant, and the grocers the Garden of Eden. Plays were performed on mobile pageant wagons, decorated by the guilds to look like the proper backdrop for the story. In some cases, the pageant wagons would move from station to station performing the same play. In others, the wagons would be in a central location, with one performance at a time.

What may be most surprising for modern people is that these plays based on holy themes did not restrict themselves to what we might now consider respectful language or action. The *Noah* play performed in Wakefield, England, is particularly shocking in that Noah and his wife are frequently arguing, cussing at, and even hitting, each other. Although we tend to separate this kind of humour from sacred performances now, medieval people didn't see a problem in representing humanity at its best and worst. It was an increasingly common practice to meditate on Jesus' human nature, and thereby humanity in all its messy, earthy glory. After all, if people as flawed and irreverent as Noah and his wife could be saved, the audience could be, too.

Did they listen to music?

Absolutely. Music was such an essential part of medieval life that it was one of the seven subjects taught in school, while subjects like history and geography were not (although they could be snuck in through the side door in grammar classes). In fact, Western musical notation was first developed in the Middle Ages.

Perhaps the most famous form of medieval music known to the modern world is Gregorian chant, named after the pope who was once thought to have standardised the form. Chanting and singing were a vital part of the everyday liturgy, not just for people in monasteries and convents, but for regular Christians, too. The sound of traditional evensong which can still be heard in some European medieval cathedrals is extremely moving and haunting, as the voices carry up into the vast, vaulted ceilings.

Outside of the cathedral, musicians played a variety of woodwind and stringed instruments, as well as percussion. Brass instruments also existed, including an early version of the trombone which was (unflatteringly) called a sackbut. Trumpets were required for the fanfares needed to announce important people, especially at great events like tournaments and feasts. Recorders were popular and came in different sizes, depending on whether the musician was looking for a high or low pitch. As anyone who's ever heard a children's concert knows, playing a recorder musically requires both skill and practice, so those who made their living as musicians had definitely put in the hours.

Probably the most emblematic instrument of the Middle Ages we see today is the lute, a pear-shaped instrument with strings, strummed like a guitar. Lutes were good instruments for minstrels to carry with them, as (like guitars) they allowed singers to accompany themselves with chords as well as to pick out melodies. Lutes were also relatively light and, of course, portable. Harps were an earlier and more traditional instrument for travelling minstrels, and were especially associated with folk and bardic traditions, as in Ireland and Wales.

Minstrels were not simply musicians, but well-rounded entertainers with skills from acrobatic tricks to magic tricks, juggling, storytelling, and cracking jokes. By one thirteenth-century account, a real minstrel is one who can 'speak and rhyme well, be witty, know the story of Troy, balance apples on the points of knives, juggle, jump through hoops, play the citole, mandora, harp, fiddle [and] psaltry' and also train animals. Much like being a musician or street performer today, a minstrel needed to keep his ears open for opportunities to perform, such as the regular circuits of fairs, market days, and festivals; otherwise, there were many times where he was at risk of literally singing for his supper. Their itinerant lives made them knowledgeable about the countryside, which is why they also made excellent messengers – and sources of news.

> One of Henry II's favourite entertainers, Roland le Pettour, was given 30 acres of land on the sole condition that every Christmas he perform his signature trick for the king: a leap, a whistle, and a fart.

A minstrel who wanted more stability could get a job as a town 'wait', paid a small amount annually to be on call for whenever the community needed music, like parades, celebrations, and plays. Waits could also be hired out by private citizens for weddings and funerals. Because they were required to perform in both wide-open and intimate spaces, waits were required to be skilled with both loud instruments (like trumpets and shawms) and soft ones (like harps).

Troubadours were unlike minstrels in that they were typically attached to one person's court for an extended period of time, and their job included writing and performing not only entertaining songs, but also songs of flattery and praise for their patrons and patronesses. They considered themselves musicians and poets, and would have been insulted to be asked to fart on command (although maybe not if 30 acres of land was involved).

Couture, Competition, and Courtly Love 113

> The troubadour tradition started out in the south of France, where Duke William of Aquitaine (grandfather of Eleanor) wrote his own songs about his virility and his conquests in the bedroom.

In a formula that will be familiar to anyone listening to modern radio, troubadours' songs tended to involve the singer being in love with a near-perfect, beautiful, yet unattainable lady, usually one in a relationship with another man. The love felt by the singer is extremely painful, to the point at which death might be preferable. The lady is described as cruel for not allowing her suitor to enjoy the pleasures of her body in secret despite her social and marital obligations.

The popularity of this music touched off a new cultural movement called 'fin'amors' or 'courtly love' that spread from music to literature, to fashion, to courtesy. Chivalry, in which a woman of great beauty and virtue is placed on a pedestal to be won by a man of great honour and prowess, comes out of this tradition, and the remnants of courtly love still exist in songs, books, movies, and 'old-fashioned manners' such as holding doors open for women.

Did they play games?

Yes! In fact, some of the board games, dice games, and even card games we play today were also played in the Middle Ages.

Dice games were popular, especially among soldiers, since dice were infinitely portable, and the fast pace of the games made it easy to bet on them. Dice could be made of wood, bone, or ivory, and many, many medieval dice have survived, including weighted ones for cheating. As the church disapproved of gambling, it also disapproved of dice games.

One medieval board game still played today is backgammon, while another is nine men's morris. Chess, invented in India, reached medieval Europe via the Middle East. The pieces on the chessboard were altered from the original form, however, so that the European version no longer has pieces like elephants; it has castles, knights, and bishops instead. Some of the oldest European chess pieces were discovered washed up on a beach on the Isle of Lewis in Scotland, having been lovingly carved from walrus ivory.

A complete set of medieval playing cards, some of which are on display at the Met Cloisters Museum in New York, shows kings, queens, knaves (jacks), and numbered cards of different suits, although the suits are not the familiar hearts, clubs, spades, and diamonds of most modern cards. Instead, the suits are made of equipment and tack used in horsemanship and hunting. Because they are lavishly illustrated, these were definitely not owned by peasants, and it's likely that card games were the domain of the elite until the mass manufacture of paper and the invention of the printing press.

Finally, there were outdoor games to play, like quoits (an early form of horseshoes), boules (similar to pétanque or bocce), and pell mell (an early form of croquet).

Did they play any sports?

Medieval people definitely enjoyed sports, and we know a little bit about the sports they played from Edward III of England's ban on playing all sports on holidays except for archery. It says, 'people take to the throwing of stones, wood, and iron; and some to hand-ball, foot-ball, and stick-play'. These first sports were probably similar to highland games and modern track and field.

As now, football ('soccer' in North America) was widely played in Europe, with balls that were made from either the inflated bladders of pigs or from leather stuffed with moss. People also played tennis and badminton, and an early form of golf called 'colf'.

Sometimes called 'the sport of kings', falconry or hawking was widely practiced across Europe in the Middle Ages, and a well-stocked mews was a sign of both sophistication and status. Unlike hunting, hawking meant the thrill of the chase without the inconvenience of getting down from the horse or having any especial prowess or gruelling physical training. It also meant a ride out in the forest among your fellow aristocrats without the chaperoning and eavesdropping possible in close quarters. It's no wonder that the language of falconry made its way into medieval love poetry.

Hunting was also an enjoyable and often-practiced sport among the aristocracy. Usually, hunters used dogs to flush out prey, although the kill was meant to be made by humans. Deer and boar were the most frequent quarry, and both were potentially dangerous to the hunters: stags' antlers were nothing to be trifled with, and boars' tusks were even more dangerous, as the height of a boar made it likely that its tusks could cut the hunter's femoral artery. King or commoner, death would occur in minutes.

Despite the danger (or perhaps because of it), hunting was so loved and enjoyed by kings that great swathes of land were reserved for royal hunting – no one else was allowed to hunt in the royal forests unless given express permission. Naturally, this was an unfair and unpopular law in a time during which food was already difficult to come by. Regardless, poaching was a severe offense, punishable by execution or by being outlawed, as some versions of the Robin Hood legend demonstrate.

What about tournaments?

Tournaments came into existence in the twelfth century and, believe it or not, were not initially focused on the joust. Early tournaments focused on mêlées, instead: large battles in which knights were divided into two different teams that fought for supremacy on a field. Combatants started out on horseback and were meant to be knocked to the ground, continuing the fight on foot.

> The word tournament comes from French *'torner'*: to turn. It describes the action of turning to face new opponents in the mêlée.

Although mêlées were not actually meant to be as dangerous as combat, the vast number of people and horses in a small space bashing each other with blunted weapons was still a recipe for disaster. Many men died either in tournaments, or afterwards from injuries they sustained in combat or by being trampled by immense warhorses. One of Henry II and Eleanor of Aquitaine's sons, Geoffrey, died in a mêlée, clearing the way for John to become king after Richard the Lionheart's death.

Being captured in a tournament meant more than just being shown up by another knight and embarrassed; it meant having to pay your captor a ransom, often your horse. More important people could fetch bigger ransoms, which is why knights sometimes ganged up on each other. In one tournament, William Marshal, one of the most famous knights of the Middle Ages, had to fend off five attackers at once. People captured in the mêlée were corralled and only allowed to return to the battle on a promise to pay their ransom, although some unchivalrous types did sneak back onto the field anyway.

As the years went on, tournaments changed, moving away from great battles to focus on jousting, for safety reasons. Rather than hundreds of knights knocking each other off their horses, the field narrowed down to two knights knocking each other off their horses. Tournament lances were increasingly blunted, as no one wanted to lose another heir to the throne (and perhaps inadvertently allow another John to come into power). Lances were long – up to 18 ft – and very heavy, so wielding them required both strength and skill.

People came from all over to attend tournaments, with tent cities popping up close by the field to house the competitors, their retinues, and anyone who could make money off of the tournament: food vendors, armourers, blacksmiths, tailors, and leatherworkers, among others. One important group of people to be found on the tournament circuit was ladies. The culture of chivalry and courtly love made it important not only for 'manly' men to perform glorious deeds, but also for these deeds to be witnessed by beautiful women. Tournaments, complained one theologian, allowed way too much frivolity of this sort:

> There is plenty of the seventh deadly sin, called Lust, since the tournament goers are out to entice shameless women, if they achieve prowess in arms; they are also accustomed to carry certain female tokens, as if they were their banners.

Despite clerical complaints, the culture of courtly love romanticised tournaments and helped to give them a central place in European culture right up until the end of the Middle Ages, and even beyond.

Did anyone read for pleasure?

Medieval people read widely across genres both to learn and to enjoy themselves. Most medieval books are actually miscellanies; that is, between the covers lies a whole range of texts from biographies, to recipes, to saints' lives, to explanations of certain parts of spiritual doctrine. As such, they are a fascinating glimpse into the minds of the compilers, giving us a portrait of their interests or their families'.

> What modern people call a book – that is, with pages between two covers – is technically called a codex. This is to differentiate it from the other things we also call 'books': long texts that could be written on a scroll (like the Book of Genesis).

Although literacy rates among the general population of medieval Europe were nothing compared to today's, many people did know how to read. Unlike today, however, reading wasn't normally a silent activity in the Middle Ages. People read aloud to each other as entertainment if they had the books and the skill, and listeners absorbed these stories and retold them orally. This meant that one person reading out of a book could spread that story – especially if it was a good one exponentially.

Like medieval readers, we can learn a lot about what life was through medieval biographies, which is why they were (and still so popular. William Marshal's, Boucicaut's, and even the inf Ulrich von Liechtenstein's biographies were copied and reco allow people to live vicariously through the lives of their fa famed knights, learning about chivalry and honour, as well as In what might be the first female autobiography, *The Book of Kempe*, Margery reveals many interesting details of life as wife, pilgrim, and mystic in the fifteenth century in her chronicle her divine experiences and visions, as well as the of life as a mystic.

Margery's description of her pilgrimage to Jerusale medieval readers' interest in hearing more about the w their doorsteps, too. Like modern travel literature, medieval travel literature like *The Travels of Marco Polo* brought the wide world into view, as well as both recommending good places to visit and warning of some of the challenges that could be faced along the way. For people who might never make such epic pilgrimages or journeys, the appeal was that it brought them as close as possible to being there.

In a similar vein, bestiaries contained descriptions of animals from far and wide, written in an explanatory manner to help Christians better understand the world. For example, the entry for 'pelican' talks about how the pelican will wound its own breast to feed its young with its blood. This was connected to Jesus' sacrifice, and pelicans with blood on their chests became a popular symbol for devout Christians. Beavers, on the other hand, were described as swimmers whose oil was used for medicinal purposes. Because beavers knew this, when humans approached, they were said to chew off their own testicles and throw them at the pursuers. This is why, it's explained, their Latin name is *castor*. Bestiaries were extremely popular, bizarre as we may find them today.

The faithful frequently read, carried, and gave books of hours, which contained prayers and readings related to the canonical hours of the day. In addition, people read the medieval version of 'self-help' books: instructional treatises meant to help readers live more virtuous lives and attain heaven after they died. Christine de Pizan's *Book of the Three Virtues*, for example, instructed French women on what their roles were as women, and how to be successful in life. *The Book of Chivalry*, written by the thirteenth-century Spanish author Ramon Lull, taught knights how to be more perfect, both as fighters and as men.

At the crossroads of religious literature and adventure stories were hagiographies: saints' lives. As we saw in Chapter Five, hagiography satisfied the requirements of religious literature, in that the saints inevitably remained devout, attained heaven, and converted large numbers of pagans in the process. At the same time, these stories contained images of nudity, sexuality, and gore that rival 'edgy' modern television shows. Saints' bodies – especially women's – were described

Couture, Competition, and Courtly Love   119

in great detail, from the quality of their skin and hair, to the degree of nakedness involved in the torture inflicted by the sinful pagans. Their wounds and methods of torture were also vividly described, from blood and cuts, to broken bones, to burns and beheadings. As with plays, however, the addition of sex and violence was not seen as blasphemous, but merely as another exploration of the human suffering so central to medieval Christianity.

Adventure stories outside of hagiography were, of course, just as popular. The Viking sagas, in particular, have everything a reader or listener could want: travel, magic, love, dirty jokes, fighting, and singing. The sagas sometimes had their roots in what may be the lives of real people like Erik the Red and Ragnar Loðbrok, still famous for their travels and their courage. Celtic stories, like those found in *The Mabinogion* were written down, too, keeping their unique blend of the supernatural and the natural from being completely steamrolled by other literature.

Finally, there were the romances. Romances became increasingly popular after the twelfth century, and their telling and retelling helped to spread the culture of courtly love from southern France across the continent. These stories, like the sagas and Celtic folk tales, often had a supernatural element to them, a brave (usually named) knight or prince, and a beautiful (usually unnamed) damsel, trapped and in need of rescue. Unlike early Norse and Celtic literature, which tends to stem from oral tales, continental romances were increasingly written before they were told. Arthurian romances were some of the most popular medieval tales of all, as they continue to be today.

> 'Romance' originally meant a story told in one of the romance languages (French, Italian, Spanish, or Portuguese – languages derived from the Roman language: Latin). Some of the most popular stories centred around courtly love relationships, however, which is why love stories are still called romances.

Just like today, everyone in medieval Europe had a hobby, interest, or a way to pass the time outside of the way they made a living, whether it was playing football or playing music. When so many depictions of medieval people show them in sadness, anger, or fear, it's important to picture them in these moments of leisure, too, among family and friends, enjoying peaceful moments and laughter together. Looking at the many trials of medieval life, it's easy to forget just how much joy people found in the everyday pleasures of free time spent together.

A Final Word

Medieval Europe was an endlessly fascinating moment in time and space: an unforgettable convergence of religious belief and romantic ideals that can never be cleverly summed up into a neat sentence. Over a thousand years of wonderfully diverse and rich history means there's always more to learn and explore, and no history book is ever truly finished.

What can be said for certain about the people of medieval Europe, however, is that they did wish to be remembered. Monuments, chronicles, and the quiet requests for prayers carefully handwritten at the end of thousand-year-old manuscripts show just how important it was to the people of the past that we try our best to remember them, and to see them as they were in all their human weakness and strength. Though we can never truly know what it was like to walk in their fashionably pointed shoes, may we always strive to remember them as people with hearts and minds as curious and complicated as our own.

Acknowledgements

The process of writing a book is so much bigger than an author and an idea. My most heartfelt thanks go out to all the people who were a part of this particular journey, and all the roads that led me here.

Thank you to Eleri Pipien, whose similar thinking led her to my virtual door, and me through this one. Thanks to Claire Hopkins, Janet Brookes, Karyn Burnham, and everyone at Pen & Sword History who helped make this book the best it could be.

Thanks to the worldwide and ever-growing community of historians who have taught me so much, and who have been so tremendously kind and supportive of my work. You are too numerous to count, but please know that I smile whenever I see your names on my shelves or in my newsfeed.

Thank you to my stellar friends and my endlessly supportive family who never once doubted that this book would be a real thing someday (even when I did), who gave me moral support and tea, and who took my kids on adventures so I could write. Thanks to those people I can always count on to spread the word whenever I have a new idea or a new project on the go. Your love and support mean the world.

Thank you to my girls, who gave me time, space, quiet, and hugs enough to write. Though you be but little, you are fierce, amazing souls, and I could not be prouder of you.

Thank you seems inadequate for the gratitude I owe to Dan, whose love and generosity made it possible for me to follow this dream.

And finally, thank you to you, reader, for supporting me, and for supporting history.

Bibliography

Aberth, John. *The Black Death: The Great Mortality of 1348–1350, A Brief History with Documents.* New York: Palgrave MacMillan, 2005.

Abu-Asab, Mones, Hakima Amri, and Marc S. Micozzi. *Avicenna's Medicine: A New Translation of the 11th-Century Canon with Practical Applications for Integrative Health Care.* Rochester, VT: Healing Arts Press, 2013.

Abulafia, Anna Sapir. 'The Jews' in *A Social History of England*, edited by Julia Crick and Elizabeth Van Houts, 256-264. Cambridge: Cambridge UP, 2011.

Allen, S.J. *An Introduction to the Crusades.* Toronto: University of Toronto Press, 2017.

Anderson, Trevor. 'Dental Treatment in Medieval England.' *British Dental Journal* 197 (October 2004): 419–425.

Archibald, Elizabeth P. *Ask the Past: Pertinent and Impertinent Advice from Yesteryear.* New York: Hachette Books, 2015.

Ashenburg, Katherine. *The Dirt on Clean: An Unsanitized History.* Toronto: Vintage Canada, 2008.

Assis, Yom Tov. *Jewish Economy in the Medieval Crown of Aragon, 1213–1327: Money and Power.* Leiden, The Netherlands: E.J. Brill, 1997.

Baker, William Joseph. *Sports in the Western World*, Revised edition. Chicago: University of Illinois Press, 1988.

Barrett, W.P. 'The Trial of Jeanne D'Arc Translated into English From the Original Latin and French Documents.' *Medieval Sourcebook.*

Fordham University. Accessed 31 July 2018. https://sourcebooks.fordham.edu/basis/joanofarc-trial.asp

Barrow, Julia. *The Clergy in the Medieval World: Secular Clerics, Their Families and Careers in North-Western Europe, c.800–c.1200*. Cambridge: Cambridge UP, 2016.

Bednarski, Steven. *A Poisoned Past: The Life and Times of Margarida de Portu, A Fourteenth-Century Accused Poisoner*. Toronto: University of Toronto Press, 2014.

Benedict, Saint. *The Rule of St Benedict*. Edited and translated by Bruce L. Venarde. Cambridge, MA: Dumbarton Oaks Medieval Library, 2011.

Bennett, Matthew, Jim Bradbury, Kelly DeVries, Iain Dickie, and Phyllis Jestice. *Fighting Techniques of the Medieval World, AD 500 – AD 1500: Equipment, Combat Skills, and Tactics*. New York: Thomas Dunne Books, 2005.

Bevington, David. *Medieval Drama*. Boston, MA: Houghton Mifflin Company, 1975.

Boissoneault, Lorraine. 'How Humble Moss Healed the Wounds of Thousands in World War I', Smithsonian.com (April 28, 2017). https://www.smithsonianmag.com/science-nature/how-humble-moss-helped-heal-wounds-thousands-WWI-180963081/

British Library, 'Pope Innocent III'. Accessed 11 August 2018. https://www.bl.uk/people/pope-innocent-iii

Britnell, Richard. 'Town Life'. In *A Social History of England, 1200-1500*, edited by Rosemary Horrox and W. Mark Ormrod. Cambridge: Cambridge UP, 2006: 134–178.

Brown, Nancy Marie. *Ivory Vikings: The Mystery of the Most Famous Chessmen in the World and the Woman who Made Them*. New York: St Martin's Press, 2015.

Burger, Michael. *Sources for the History of Western Civilization: From Antiquity to the Mid-Eighteenth Century*, Vol. 1, 2nd Ed. Toronto: University of Toronto Press, 2015.

Butler, Sarah M. '"I Will Never Consent to be Wedded with You!": Coerced Marriage in the Courts of Medieval England.' *Canadian Journal of History* 39 (August 2004): 247–270.

Cappellanus, Andreas. *The Art of Courtly Love*, translated by John Jay Parry. New York: W.W. Norton and Co., 1969.

Carlson, Bob. 'Crawling Through the Millenia: Maggots and Leeches Come Full Circle.' *Biotechnology Healthcare* 3 no. 1 (February 2006): 14, 17.

Castor, Helen. *Joan of Arc: A History*. London: Faber and Faber, 2014.

Caxton, William. 'Prologue and Epilogue to the 1485 Edition' in Sir Thomas Malory, *Le Morte Darthur*, edited by Stephen H.A. Shepherd. New York: W.W. Norton and Company, 2004, 814–818.

Chaucer, Geoffrey. 'The General Prologue' in *The Riverside Chaucer*, 3rd ed., edited by Larry D. Benson. New York: Houghton Mifflin Company, 1987.

Clark, Anna. *Desire: A History of European Sexuality*. New York: Routledge, 2008.

Coatsworth, Elizabeth, and Gale R. Owen-Crocker. *Clothing the Past: Surviving Garments from Early Medieval to Early Modern Western Europe*. Boston: Brill, 2017.

Coulton, G.G. *Social Life in Britain from the Conquest to the Reformation*. Cambridge: Cambridge UP, 1918.

Crosby, Alfred W. *Throwing Fire: Projectile Technology Through History*. Cambridge: Cambridge UP, 2002.

Crouch, David. *Tournament*. London: Hambledon and Continuum, 2005.

Cuffel, Alexandra. 'Polemicizing Women's Bathing Among Medieval and Early Modern Muslims and Christians.' In *The Nature and Function of Water, Baths, Bathing and Hygiene from Antiquity through the Renaissance*, edited by Cynthia Kosso and Anne Scott. Leiden, The Netherlands: Brill, 2009.

De Curzon, Henri. *La Règle du Temple.* Paris: Société de L'Histoire de France, 1886.

De Pizan, Christine. *The Selected Writings of Christine de Pizan*, translated by Renate Blumenfeld-Kosinski and Kevin Brownlee. Edited by Renate Blumenfeld-Kosinski. New York: W.W. Norton and Company, 1997.

DeVries, Kelly. *Joan of Arc: A Military Leader.* Thrupp, UK: Sutton Publishing, 2003.

De Ridder-Symoens, Hilde, ed. *A History of the University in Europe, Volume I: Universities in the Middle Ages.* Cambridge: Cambridge UP, 1992.

Dubin, Nathaniel E., trans. *The Fabliaux: A New Verse Translation.* New York: Liveright Publishing Corporation, 2013.

Everett, Nicholas. *The Alphabet of Galen: Pharmacy from Antiquity to the Middle Ages.* Toronto: University of Toronto Press, 2012.

Fordham University. 'The Questioning of John Rykener, A Male Cross-Dressing Prostitute, 1395.' *Medieval Sourcebook.* Accessed 1 August 2018. https://sourcebooks.fordham.edu/source/1395rykener.asp

Fordham University. 'Twelfth Ecumenical Council: Lateran IV, 1215.' *Medieval Sourcebook.* Accessed 11 August 2018. https://sourcebooks.fordham.edu/basis/lateran4.asp

Frankopan, Peter. *The Silk Roads: A New History of the World.* New York: Vintage Books, 2017.

Frohne, Bianca. 'Performing Dis/ability? Constructions of "Infirmity" in Late Medieval and Early Modern Life Writing' in *Infirmity in Antiquity and the Middle Ages: Social and Cultural Approaches to Health, Weakness and Care*, edited by Christian Krötzl, Katariina Mustakallio and Jenni Kuuliala. New York: Routledge, 2015, 51-66.

Geary, Patrick J. *Readings in Medieval History.* Peterborough, Canada: Broadview, 1989.

Gilchrist, Roberta. *Medieval Life: Archaeology and the Life Course.* Woodbridge, UK: Boydell, 2012.

Glick, Thomas, Steven J. Livesey, and Faith Wallis, eds. *Medieval Science, Technology, and Medicine: An Encyclopedia.* New York: Routledge, 2005.

Goldberg, P.J.P. 'The Fashioning of Bourgeois Domesticity in Later Medieval England: A Material Culture Perspective' in *Medieval Domesticity: Home, Housing and Household in Medieval England*, edited by Maryanne Kowaleski and P.J.P. Godlberg. Cambridge: Cambridge UP, 2008, 124-144.

Gravett, Christopher. *Knight: Noble Warrior of England 1200–1600.* Oxford: Osprey Publishing, 2008.

Green, Monica, ed. *The Trotula: An English Translation of the Medieval Compendium of Women's Medicine.* Philadelphia: University of Pennsylvania Press, 2002.

Gregg, Joan Young. *Devils, Women, and Jews: Reflections of the Other in Medieval Sermon Stories.* New York: State University of New York Press, 1997.

Halliwell, James Orchard. *The Book of Curtasye: An English Poem of the Fourteenth Century.* London: C. Richards, 1841.

Hindley, Geoffrey. *Medieval Sieges and Siegecraft.* New York: Skyhorse Publishing, 2009.

Horn, Walter and Ernest Born. 'Heaven on Earth: The Plan of St Gall'. *The Wilson Quarterly* 4, no.1 (Winter 1980): 171–179.

Hsy, Jonathan. 'Disability.' *The Cambridge Companion to The Body in Literature*, edited by David Hillman and Ulrika Maude, 24–20. New York: Cambridge UP, 2015.

Jacob, H.E. *Six Thousand Years of Bread: Its Holy and Unholy History.* New York, Skyhorse Publishing, 2007.

Jager, Eric. *The Last Duel: A True Story of Crime, Scandal, and Trial by Combat in Medieval France.* New York: Broadway Books, 2004.

Janin, Hunt. *Medieval Justice: Cases and Laws in France, England, and Germany, 500–1500.* Jefferson, NC: McFarland and Company, 2004.

Jeay, Madeline and Kathleen Garay, eds. *The Distaff Gospels.* Peterborough, ON: Broadview, 2006.

Jones, Dan. *Magna Carta: The Making and Legacy of the Great Charter.* London: Head of Zeus Ltd., 2014.

Jones, Dan. *The Templars: The Rise and Spectacular Fall of God's Holy Warriors.* New York: Viking, 2017.

Karras, Ruth Mazo. *Common Women: Prostitution and Sexuality in Medieval England.* Oxford: Oxford UP, 1996.

Karras, Ruth Mazo. *Sexuality in Medieval Europe: Doing Unto Others.* New York: Routledge, 2005.

Keene, Derek. 'Issues of Water in Medieval London to c.1300.' *Urban History* 28, no.2 (2001): 161–179.

Kennedy, Kathleen E. 'Gripping it by the Husk: The Medieval English Coconut.' *The Medieval Globe* 3.1 (2017): 1–26.

Kerr, Julie. *Life in the Medieval Cloister.* London: Continuum, 2009.

Krug, Ilana. '*Sotelties* and Politics: The Message Behind the Food in Late Medieval Feasts.' Paper presented at the International Congress on Medieval Studies, Kalamazoo, MI, Friday, 11 May 2018.

Kucher, Michael. 'The Use of Water and its Regulation in Medieval Siena.' *Journal of Urban History* 31, no.4 (May 2005): 504–536.

Le Ménagier de Paris. *The Good Wife's Guide: A Medieval Household Book*, translated by Gina L. Greco and Christine M. Rose. Ithaca, NY: Cornell UP, 2009.

Lee, John S. *The Medieval Clothier.* Woodbridge, UK: The Boydell Press, 2018.

Longman, William. *The History of the Life and Times of Edward the Third*, volume II. London: Longmans, Green and Co., 1869.

Loengard, Janet S. '"Which May be Said to be Her Own": Widows and Goods in Late-Medieval England.' In *Medieval Domesticity: Home, Housing and Household in Medieval England*, edited by Maryanne Kowaleski and P.J.P Goldbery, 162–176. Cambridge: Cambridge UP, 2008.

Luria, Maxwell S. and Richard L. Hoffman. *Middle English Lyrics: Authoritative Texts, Critical and Historical Backgrounds, Perspectives on Six Poems*. New York: W.W. Norton and Company, 1974.

March, Ausiàs. *Ausiàs March: Verse Translations of Thirty Poems*, translated and edited by Robert Archer. Woodbridge, UK: The Boydell Press, 2006.

Medievalists.net. 'Did People in the Middle Ages Take Baths?' 13 April 2013. http://www.medievalists.net/2013/04/did-people-in-the-middle-ages-take-baths/

Meens, Rob. 'Penitential Varieties' in *The Oxford Handbook of Medieval Christianity*, edited by John H. Arnold. Oxford: Oxford UP, 2014, 254–270.

Merback, Mitchell B. *The Thief, the Cross, and the Wheel: Pain and the Spectacle of Punishment in Medieval and Renaissance Europe*. London: Reaktion Books, Ltd., 1999.

Metzler, Irina. *Fools and Idiots? Intellectual Disability in the Middle Ages*. Manchester: Manchester UP, 2016.

Mills, Robert. *Suspended Animation: Pain, Pleasure and Punishment in Medieval Culture*. London: Reaktion Books, Ltd. 2005.

Montanari, Massimo. *Medieval Tastes: Food, Cooking, and the Table*, translated by Beth Archer Brombert. New York: Columbia UP, 2015.

Moore, John. *Pope Innocent III and his World*. Brookfield, VT: Ashgate, 1999.

Morris, Marc. *A Great and Terrible King: Edward I and the Forging of Britain*. London: Windmill Books, 2008.

Mount, Toni. *Dragon's Blood and Willow Bark: The Mysteries of Medieval Medicine.* Stroud, UK: Amberley Publishing, 2015.

Murray, Alexander. *Suicide in the Middle Ages: Volume II: The Curse on Self-Murder.* Oxford: Oxford UP, 2000.

Newman, Paul B. *Daily Life in the Middle Ages.* Jefferson, North Carolina: McFarland & Co., 2001.

Newman, Paul B. *Growing Up in the Middle Ages.* Jefferson, North Carolina: McFarland & Co., 2007.

Newman, Paul B. *Travel and Trade in the Middle Ages.* Jefferson, North Carolina: McFarland & Co., 2011.

Norwegian Institute for Cultural Heritage Research. 'Unusual Medieval Dice Found in Bergen.' Accessed August 9, 2018. https://niku.no/en/2018/03/uvanlig-terning-middelalderen-funnet-bergen/

Nutz, Beatrix. 'Medieval Lingerie Discovered.' Universität Innsbruck, accessed 1 August 2018. https://www.uibk.ac.at/ipoint/news/2012/buestenhalter-aus-dem-mittelalter.html.en

Orme, Nicholas. *Medieval Children.* New Haven, CT: Yale UP, 2001.

Oxford English Dictionary. 'Friday', accessed 1 August 2018. https://en.oxforddictionaries.com/definition/thursday

Oxford English Dictionary. 'Monday', accessed 1 August 2018. https://en.oxforddictionaries.com/definition/monday

Oxford English Dictionary. 'Saturday', accessed 1 August 2018. https://en.oxforddictionaries.com/definition/saturday

Oxford English Dictionary. 'Sunday', accessed 1 August 2018. https://en.oxforddictionaries.com/definition/sunday

Oxford English Dictionary. 'Thursday', accessed 1 August 2018. https://en.oxforddictionaries.com/definition/thursday

Oxford English Dictionary. 'Tuesday', accessed 1 August 2018. https://en.oxforddictionaries.com/definition/tuesday

Oxford English Dictionary. 'Wednesday', accessed 1 August 2018. https://en.oxforddictionaries.com/definition/wednesday

Paden, William D. and Frances Freeman Paden. *Troubadour Poems from the South of France*. Cambridge, UK: D.S. Brewer, 2007.

Partington, J.R. *A History of Greek Fire and Gunpowder*. Baltimore, MD: 1999.

Puff, Helmut. *Sodomy in Reformation Germany and Switzerland: 1400–1600*. Chicago: University of Chicago Press, 2003.

Rawcliffe, Carole. 'A Marginal Occupation? The Medieval Laundress and her Work.' *Gender and History* 21, no.1 (April 2009): 147–169.

Rawcliffe, Carole. *Urban Bodies: Communal Health in Late Medieval English Towns and Cities*. Woodbridge, UK: Boydell, 2013.

Rebora, Giovanni. *Culture of the Fork: A Brief History of Food in Europe*, translated by Albert Sonnenfeld. New York: Columbia UP, 2001.

Riddle, John M. *Eve's Herbs: A History of Contraception and Abortion in the West*. Cambridge, MA: Harvard University Press, 1997.

Roberts, Charlotte and Keith Manchester. *The Archaeology of Disease*, third ed. Ithaca, NY: Cornell UP, 2005.

Scott, Margaret. *Fashion in the Middle Ages*. Los Angeles: J. Paul Getty Museum, 2011.

Singer, Julie. *Blindness and Therapy in Late Medieval French and Italian Poetry*. Cambridge: D.S. Brewer, 2011.

Singman, Jeffrey L. *Daily Life in Medieval Europe*. Westport, CT: Greenwood Press, 1999.

Skinner, Patricia, ed. *The Jews in Medieval Britain: Historical, Literary and Archaeological Perspectives*. Woodbridge, UK: Boydell, 2003.

Somerville, Angus A. and R. Andrew McDonald. *The Viking Age: A Reader*. Toronto: University of Toronto Press, 2014.

Southworth, John. *The English Medieval Minstrel.* Woodbridge, UK: The Boydell Press, 1989.

Taylor, Craig and Jane H.M. Taylor, trans. *The Chivalric Biography of Boucicaut, Jean II Le Meingre.* Woodbridge, UK: The Boydell Press, 2016.

Than, Ker. 'Maggots and Leeches: Old Medicine is New.' *Live Science* (April 19, 2005). https://www.livescience.com/203-maggots-leeches-medicine.html

Theodore of Tarsus. 'The Penitential of Theodore' in *Medieval Handbooks of Penance: A Translation of the Principal* Libres Poenitentiales *and Selections from Related Documents*, translated by John Thomas McNeill and Helena M. Gamer. New York: Columbia UP, 1938. 182-214.

Trio, Paul. 'Ypres and the Drinking-Water Problem.' In *Urban Space in the Middle Ages and the Early Modern Age*, edited by Albrecht Classen. Berlin: Walter de Gruyter, 2009.

Tracy, Larissa. *Torture and Brutality in Medieval Literature: Negotiations of National Identity.* Cambridge: D.S. Brewer, 2012.

Vela, Carles. 'Defining "Apothecary" in the Medieval Crown of Aragon.' In *Medieval Urban Identity: Health, Economy and Regulation*, edited by Flocel Sabaté, 127–142. Newcastle upon Tyne, UK: Cambridge Scholars Publishing, 2015.

Vigarello, Georges. *Concepts of Cleanliness: Changing Attitudes in France Since the Middle Ages.* Translated by Jean Birrell. Cambridge: Cambridge UP, 2008.

Wallis, Faith, ed. *Medieval Medicine: A Reader.* Toronto: University of Toronto Press, 2010.

Notes

Chapter 1: A Dirty Little Secret

For this chapter, I'm especially indebted to the painstaking work of Carole Rawcliffe, whose work on laundry and urban cleanliness heavily informs those sections (please see 'Marginal' and *Urban*). For the example of the London stews being shut down for immorality, please see Karras (*Common*); for drainage in Ypres, see Trio; for Siena, see Kucher; for toothpaste, see Anderson; for the monks of Cluny, see Kerr.

Chapter 2: Farming, Fasting, Feasting

Although this chapter briefly touches on the racial diversity of medieval Europe via trade routes, I'd encourage readers to delve much further into the excellent research being done by many scholars on this today. A good place to start is People of Color in European Art History (https://medievalpoc.tumblr.com). For chestnut bread, see Montanari; for the poem on table manners, see Halliwell. For the wedding *sotelties* mentioned here, my thanks to Ilana Krug for allowing me to refer to her ICMS paper.

Chapter 3: The Art of Love

The Towton spur, the bridal girdle, and the thimbles and pottery shards in this chapter can be found in Gilchrist's *Medieval Life*. Much of what we know about medieval sexuality comes from the work of Ruth Mazo Karras, and her work has been hugely influential on me. For the investigation into a husband's impotence, see *Common Women*; for the knights buried together, for Hetzeldorfer, Ronchaia, and Rykener's legal cases, as well as for a more thorough discussion of LGBTQIA+ sexuality, see *Sexuality in Medieval Europe*. For contraception, including

Montaillou, the wording of confessors, and the list of contraceptive herbs, see Riddle; for the fabliaux, see Dubin; for the funerary customs mentioned here and the example of Hereford Cathedral, see Orme. My thanks to Kathleen Kennedy for letting me know about the use of coconut oil in childbirth.

Chapter 4: Nasty and Brutish

For more information on the Viking slave trade, as well as an excellent exploration of intercultural trade in general, please see Frankopan. For the definition of the word 'Viking' used here, see Somerville and McDonald. Merbeck's work on the complex attitudes towards executions has deeply informed my own; this section follows his lead as outlined in *The Thief, The Cross, and The Wheel*. For trial by combat and by ordeal, please see Janin. Margarida de Portu's trial, which I've briefly summarized here, is fully explored in Bednarski's *A Poisoned Past*. For a more thorough discussion of torture, please see Tracy; the story of Warwolf can be found in Morris.

Chapter 5: The Age of Faith

For more in-depth information on the roles of clergy and ordination, see Barrow; and for the song that asks spiritual questions, see Luria. For Jewish guilds in Aragon, see Assis; for regulations on Jewish and Muslim clothing, see Fordham's notes on Lateran IV; for a closer look at Edward I's persecution of the Jews, see Morris.

Chapter 6: In Sickness and in Health

Many of the treatments mentioned here were known and used globally by pre-modern societies. For snail slime, see Mount; for mulberry's properties, see Everett. The third burn remedy comes from *The Trotula*. Green's edition of this book is essential reading; she has traced both the authorship and the widespread use of *The Trotula* as indicated here. The full prayer to medical herbs can be found in Wallis, and for the range of apothecaries' goods and services, see Vela. Leeches and maggots are registered as medical devices by the American Food and Drug Administration. For the soldier with the iron hand, see Frohne; for hospitals for the blind, see Hsy; for a more extensive look at how medieval people dealt with cognitive disabilities and mental illness in legal terms, see Metzler.

Chapter 7: Couture, Competition, and Courtly Love

For the different colours of gowns worn by medieval doctors, see De Ridder-Symoens; for eyebrow grooming punished in hell, see Gregg. Lee's *The Medieval Clothier* provided me with the technical details of the manufacture of broadcloth, including its measurement, which is quoted here. Please see that excellent work for a closer look at the textile industry. For men's underwear, see Newman (*Daily*), and for the underwear and bras found in Austria, see Nutz. For the skills of a good minstrel, Roland le Pettour, and more on medieval waits, see Southworth; for outdoor games and sports, see Newman (*Daily*); and for everything you ever wanted to know about tournaments, including their etymology and the grouchy quote by Jacques de Vitry on lust, see Crouch.

The bibliography provided is selective, but will provide readers with many more avenues to follow. My thanks to all the scholars whose work has been so instrumental in advancing our collective knowledge, as well as my personal knowledge as reflected here.

Index

Agriculture, 9–10, 14–15, 31
Alfred the Great, 56, 77
Animals, 9–10, 14–15, 29, 65–66, 114–115, 118
Arthur, King, 38, 86, 119

Bathing, *see* Hygiene
Becket, Thomas, 60–61, 76, 83
Black Death, 48–50, 70, 88, 102–103, 106
Boucicaut (Jean II le Meingre), 67, 71, 117
Byzantine Empire, 25, 89

Castles, 12–13, 17, 20, 68–72, 97
   see also War and warfare, sieges
Chaucer, Geoffrey, 21, 82–83
Children and childhood, 4, 14, 20, 22, 26, 31–34, 36–37, 40, 43–47, 50–51, 88, 105, 107
   childbirth, 34, 43–5, 99
   pregnancy, 37–8, 43–4, 47, 100
   teenage years, 31–3, 36, 42, 47, 55, 105
Chivalry, *see* courtly love
Christianity, 2–3, 16, 21, 33, 40, 44–45, 49–52, 57–59, 75–92, 95, 110–111, 116–117
   baptism, 44–5, 50–1
   doubt, 75, 83–5, 92
   pilgrimage, 19, 82–3, 89–90, 95, 117–8
   sin and penance, 21–3, 29, 37, 39–40, 44–5, 50–2, 83, 85, 118
   see also Popes and papacy; Priests and clerics; Monasticism and monastic life
Clothing and dress, 5, 7–9, 18, 35, 40–41, 79, 87 104–110
Courtly love, 32, 38, 104, 113, 116, 119
Crusades, 7, 75–76, 89–91

De Pizan, Christine, 48, 118
Disabilities, 100–102
   blindness, 56, 95, 100–101
   cognitive impairment and mental illness, 49, 98–9, 101–102
   deafness, 56, 95, 100

Early Modern period, 4, 7, 59, 63, 73, 86, 88, 100, 103
Education and learning, 46–47, 80–81, 98–99, 105, 111, 117
Edward I, 70, 88
Edward III, 4, 34, 49, 64, 106, 114
Eleanor of Aquitaine, 113, 115

Fabliaux, 36–37, 42
Food and drink, 2, 6–7, 14–30, 44, 72, 79, 96, 98

Government and administration, 10, 33, 53, 63, 76, 79

Henry II, 60–61, 76, 112, 115
Henry V, 64, 73
Henry VII, 34, 76
Heresy and heretical movements, 40, 57, 60, 63, 85–87, 89, 91–92
Homes and houses, 1, 10–11, 16–17, 20, 22, 36, 87
Hygiene, 1–13, 25–29
Hunting, 32, 57, 114–115

Innocent III, 35, 41, 59, 65, 87, 92
Islam and Muslim life, 2–3, 22, 75, 78, 83, 87–92

Jean II le Meingre, *see* Boucicaut
Jerusalem, 78, 83, 88–91, 117
Joan of Arc, 40–41, 60, 70
John I, 4, 13, 61, 69, 115
Judaism, Jewish life, 2–3, 22, 61, 75, 87–88, 90, 92

Kempe, Margery, 117

Lateran IV, *see* Innocent III
Law and justice, 21, 56–63, 78, 101
  Magna Carta, 16, 61, 70
  punishment, 38–41, 46, 55–8, 60, 74, 93, 102
  torture, 53, 62–3, 81–2, 119
Le Menagier de Paris, 9, 17, 24–27
LGBTQIA+, *see* sexuality
London, 2, 8, 10–12, 35, 40

Manuscripts and manuscript images, 2, 19, 95, 100, 104, 107–108, 121
March, Ausiàs, 51, 84

Marriage and married life, 19, 28, 31–42, 51–52, 55, 76, 105
  adultery, 37–9, 60
  wedding, 19, 28, 35–6, 112
  widowhood, 32, 47, 81
  see also Sex and sexuality
Medicine, 3–7, 15, 20, 42–44, 47–48, 72, 80, 89, 93–103, 118
  see also Trotula, The
Monasticism and monastic life, 3–5, 8, 12, 15–17, 20–23, 39–40, 42, 52, 78–81, 90, 109, 111
  Franciscans, 23, 79, 104
  Plan of St. Gall, 3, 12, 79–80
  Rule of St. Benedict, 3, 7, 22–3, 79–80, 109
Music, 24, 28, 46, 104, 111–113
  minstrels, 111–12
  troubadours, 104, 115–16
Muslims, *see* Islam

Norse, *see* Vikings

Paris, 2, 8, 101
Philip (IV) the Fair, 39, 62, 76, 88
Pilgrimage, *see* Christianity, pilgrimage
Plague, *see* Black Death
Popes and papacy, 35, 41, 59, 65, 76, 87, 90–91
  see also Innocent III
Priests and clerics, 41–42, 78–79

Renaissance, *see* Early Modern period
Richard I, 90–91, 97, 115
Robin Hood, 57, 115

Roman Empire, 1, 19, 38, 53, 86, 98, 119

Saints, 22, 44, 55, 77–78, 81–83, 95, 117–119
  hagiography, 82, 117–19
  saints' days, 22–3, 77–8
Sex and sexuality, 2, 34, 36–43, 55, 62, 87, 99–100, 118
  clergy, 36–42
  contraception, 42–3, 99
  LGBTQIA+, 38–41
  prostitution, 2, 37, 40
Slaves and slavery, 19, 54–55, 77
Sports and games, 45–46, 64, 113–116

Templars, 39–40, 62–63, 76, 87, 90–91
Theodore, Penitential of, 21–2, 29, 40
Torture, *see* Law and justice
Tournaments, 32, 35, 66, 68, 104–105, 111, 115–116
Trade and commerce, 7, 18–19, 33, 54–55, 87–88, 108–109
  guilds and professionals, 8, 20, 47, 54, 59, 87, 108–110
  Silk Road, 19, 88

Trotula, The, 5–6, 44, 94, 99

Urban life, 9–12, 15, 17, 19–20, 35, 50, 82

Vikings, 16, 25, 54–55, 86, 119

War and warfare, 13–14, 20, 33, 47, 49–50, 63–74, 89–91, 97, 115–116
  Hundred Years' War, 63–4, 76
  knights, knighthood, 32, 41, 47, 65–8, 90, 105, 113, 115–19
  sieges, 13–4, 20, 28, 65, 68–72, 91
  weapons, 61, 64, 68–70, 72, 115
  bows and archery, 47, 64–5, 68–9, 71, 74, 97, 114
  guns and cannons, 64, 70, 73
  lances, 47, 66, 116
  swords, 47, 66, 73–4, 86, 106
Women, 5, 8, 20, 37–48, 55, 80–81, 99–100, 104–109, 113, 116, 118